Praise for *A Sweet, Wild Note*

'Well worth a read . . . hits many sweet notes'
– Mark Avery, author of *Remarkable Birds* and *Inglorious: Conflict in the Uplands*

'A delightful meditation on the wonders of nature's best free show – birdsong – and how it has seeped into our culture through the ages'
– Stephen Moss, author of *Wild Hares and Hummingbirds* and *Wild Kingdom*

'Between the fibrillating throats of birds and the human mind lies an extraordinary landscape, a place created by the intersection of culture, biology, and literature. Richard Smyth is a brilliant, insightful, and witty guide in this fascinating terrain'
– David George Haskell, author of *The Songs of Trees* and the Pulitzer finalist, *The Forest Unseen*. Professor of Biology, University of the South

'This is a delightful book that does exactly what it says on the cover: it plays a sweet wild note. If you are already tuned in to bird song you will learn a lot more and if you aren't you will want to be. Reading it honestly seems to have improved my (ornithological) listening and hearing as well as cheering my heart'
– Sara Maitland, author of *Gossip from the Forest: The Tangled Roots of Our Forests and Fairytales*

A Sweet, Wild Note

What we hear when the birds sing

Richard Smyth

For Frin

First published 2017 by
Elliott and Thompson Limited
27 John Street, London WC1N 2BX
www.eandtbooks.com

ISBN: 978-1-78396-314-0

p. 21: 'The Oven Bird', *Mountain Interval* by Robert Frost (New York: Holt, 1916);
p. 21: 'Yet Not to Listen to That Sung Nothing', *Person to Person* by John Ciardi
(New Brunswick: Rutgers University Press, 1964); p. 32: 'The Progress of Rhyme'
by John Clare, from *John Clare: Major Works*, ed. Eric Robinson and David Powell
(Oxford: Oxford University Press, 2008); p. 35: 'Syrinx', *A Silence Opens* by Amy
Clampitt (New York: Knopf, 1994); p. 36 'Widgeon', *Station Island* by Seamus Heaney
(London: Faber & Faber, 1984); p. 96: 'Oikopleura, Jelly Builder', *Larval Forms and
Other Zoological Verses* by Walter Garstang (Oxford: Blackwell, 1951); p. 157: 'Birds,
Why Are Ye Silent?' by John Clare, from *John Clare: Major Works*, ed. Eric Robinson
and David Powell (Oxford: Oxford University Press, 2008); p. 171: 'The Pike's
Song', *Ice Mirror* by Aaro Hellaakoski (Helsinki: Otava, 1928); p. 171: 'Sound of the
Axe', *Oblique Prayers* by Denise Levertov (New York: New Directions Publishing
Corporation, 1984).

9 8 7 6 5 4 3 2 1

A catalogue record for this book is available from the British Library.

Illustrations by Tim Oakenfull
Typesetting by Marie Doherty
Printed in the UK by TJ International Ltd

Contents

The language of birds is very ancient, and, like other
ancient modes of speech, very elliptical; little is said,
but much is meant and understood.
– Gilbert White, letter to Daines Barrington, September 1778

These are brand-new birds of twelve-months' growing,
Which a year ago, or less than twain,
No finches were, nor nightingales,
Nor thrushes,
But only particles of grain,
And earth, and air, and rain.

– Thomas Hardy, 'Proud Songsters' (1928)

Prologue

M y feelings about birdsong – no, my *problems* with birdsong – were crystallised for me in, appropriately enough, a tweet, one day in 2011:

> @BrianGittins1: The birds are talking to one another in their stupid language.

It was the comedian David Earl, tweeting in the guise of his alter ego Brian Gittins. It was a joke, of course. But for me, it felt liberating – like reading an article about how *Futurama* really was a better show than *The Simpsons*, or meeting someone who says that no, they don't really get Radiohead's later albums either.

My name is Richard and I was a birdsong sceptic.

I'd better explain myself. I'm a birdwatcher;* I have been, on and off, since I was little (I inherited it from my

* A birdwatcher but not, I think, a birder: that term suggests something a bit more hardcore, a bit more camo-jacketed and scope-toting and let's-go-sit-at-Spurn-Point-in-a-March-blizzard-and-see-what-turns-up (and I'm certainly not a twitcher, an elevated state of being

granddad, along with skinny ankles and a love of Test cricket). The thing was, as a kid I didn't do a great deal of actual birdwatching. In theory, I was all for it; in practice, it turned out that the countryside, once you got there, was just so full of diverting alternative pastimes (playing army, going on rope swings, falling out of trees, general fighting, shouting, etc.) that the birds didn't get a look-in. One just didn't have the time.

But I was a studious reader of nature books, field guides, the magazines sent out by the Young Ornithologists' Club – anything, really, as long as birds were involved. The nineteenth-century naturalist Charles Waterton (who lived just down the road from where I grew up in Wakefield, West Yorkshire) warned about people like me: young amateur naturalists 'who spent more time in books than in bogs'.

This explains, I think, why for a long time my experiences of the bird-life around me – the way I saw it, identified it, thought and felt about it – were missing a dimension.

When I was twelve or so, I could identify practically any bird in my bird book by sight (give or take the

that is something between an alternative lifestyle choice and an untreated neurosis).

odd wandering warbler or far-off winter gull). Here is a full list of birds I could identify by sound alone at that age:

(1) Some sort of crow
I knew a *caw* when I heard it. It meant there was definitely a crow or a rook or a jackdaw or possibly a magpie in the vicinity.

(2) (a) A woodpigeon, unless it was a collared dove
(2) (b) A collared dove, unless it was a woodpigeon
I knew a *coo*, too. It's strange to think that collared doves were unknown in the UK until the 1950s; when I was a boy, in 1980s suburbia, they were all over the place, like pale-grey pebbles balanced on roof-ridges and half-hidden in leylandii.

(3) A duck
Well, come on.

(4) A herring gull
The twanging *pyah pyah pyah* bawled from a fishing-village chimney was – and still is – the sound of a summer holiday on the Yorkshire coast, no less than the marvellous *ching, chunk, whirr* and *bleep* of Corrigan's seafront arcade in Scarborough.

(5) A peacock

Surprise entry at Number 5. Our suburban cul-de-sac was bounded on one side by Mr Andrassy's small-holding. It can only have been an acre or two, but at one time or another he kept geese, deer, guinea fowl, goats and peacocks. They were often on our back lawn, confusing the cat. Andrassy's smallholding is all houses now.

Birdsong wasn't part of my world. No, that's not quite right: it was, but – like my parents' mortgage, or the government's education policy, or the electronics of my GameBoy – I couldn't make anything of it; it didn't mean anything to me. I was shut out of the birds' conversation.*

This book is about what I'd been missing – partly, at least. It's also about what people – poets, bird fanciers, composers, film-makers, ornithologists, you, even me – have been hearing. It's about skylarks and nightingales (much harder to avoid in poetry than in real life), but it's

---

* Anyway, according to Douglas Adams in *Life, the Universe and Everything* their conversation is 'fantastically boring. It was all to do with wind speed, wing spans, power-to-weight ratios and a fair bit about berries. Unfortunately, he discovered, once you have learnt birdspeak you quickly come to realise that the air is full of it the whole time, just inane bird chatter. There is no getting away from it.'

also about magpies and wagtails, chaffinches and sparrows; it's about the tuts and sneezes of the wren, the *booee* of the starling's swanee-whistle, the blackbird's burble, the woodpigeon's somnolent *coo* ('take *two* cows, Taffy,' they're supposed to say); the squeaky hinge of the great tit, the chiffchaff's unending two-step, the jay's B-movie screams in the oak canopy. All the stuff I never really paid attention to.

The funny thing is that I wasn't alone in my cluelessness about birdsong. In 1935, the biologist Walter Garstang – of whom more later – lamented that 'the number of our countrymen and women who can pick out an individual song from the orchestra of spring and correctly identify it is extraordinarily small'. Even way back in the 1760s, the naturalist Gilbert White (one of *the* great listeners) found that the yeomen of his Hampshire village believed that the reeling call of the grasshopper warbler was made by an insect: 'The country people laugh when you tell them that it is the note of a bird.'

It's not that they didn't care, exactly. They just didn't listen.

Percy Edwards, who went on to find fame on the radio as a peerless and painstaking bird-imitator, recalled the music-hall 'bird whistlers' with whom he'd often shared a bill in the early days of his career. Many would just stick their fingers in their mouths and whistle, making a noise like no bird ever made; to impersonate a thrush, one of them told Edwards, 'I just do the same noise I do for them all.' The audiences, presumably, didn't know what sort of noise a thrush (or a skylark, or a blackbird) actually makes – but they'd still paid for a ticket. Perhaps the general idea was something along the lines of 'I don't know much about birdsong, but I know what I like.'

On the website of the University of Aberdeen's 'Listening to Birds' project – a fascinating study of our relationship with birdsong – researcher Andrew Whitehouse posts comments from members of the public recalling memorable birdsong experiences. It's wonderful: an in-their-own-words archive of how we listen to birds, and what it is we hear. One contributor remembers scraping a living as a songwriter in north London, skint and unhappy:

> Each night I would go for a long walk around Islington, and even in January of 1992–3 I could hear nightingales singing their beautiful songs. There are not many things on a bleak January night to cheer you up but I always noticed this.

It's an experience with which, I think, a lot of us can identify: the way a bright bird song on a lonely street can lift our mood, or leaven our loneliness, or bring a little bit of countryside into the brick canyons and concrete precincts of urban N5.

Only the thing is, there aren't any nightingales in Islington; there aren't any nightingales north of Egypt in January. What the skint songwriter heard were almost certainly robins. That doesn't spoil a sweet and touching story (everyone loves a robin); it just makes the point that we can have important relationships with birds' songs without knowing very much about them. Our relationships with birdsong are, as they say on Facebook, complicated. That's what this book is about.

Elsewhere in his autobiography, Percy Edwards recalls hearing a greenfinch calling *mary, mary*:

> I felt as though I'd never heard a bird before. I had, of course. They'd been chirruping away in the background all the time . . . but I'd somehow managed to shut the birds out of my consciousness. Now one had forced his way through, and suddenly my ears were opened and birdsong of every kind poured in.

I can't say it's exactly been that way for me. In the last few years I've tried to unstopper my ears and listen, really listen, to what the birds are saying. But it hasn't been about just one bird – they've all chipped in, the wrens by the river, the goldfinches chinking like a pocketful of pound coins in next door's laburnum, the sibilant dunnocks in the front yard. Best of all have been the blackcaps. The cock-blackcap is a dull grey scrap of a bird with a smart, forward-tilted black cap; it's occasionally called the 'northern nightingale',* because unlike the actual nightingale it's found north of the Humber.

I love the blackcap's song. I love it so much that I can give you a list of my top three singing blackcaps: (3) at Bingley, beside the Leeds–Skipton canal on a sunny, blustery day, perhaps three years ago, feathers fluffed, the wind spiking up his crest; (2) at Eccup reservoir one May, with the roadside foliage thick and wild; he was elusive, flitting here and there on urgent blackcap business, loosing off the song in reckless, intermittent volleys; (1) on my local patch, in ash-and-alder woodland by the Aire, intrepid on a looping stem above a hedgerow, and giving it some welly in the teeth of a bitter April wind.

---

* Historically, though, the term has been applied mainly to the song thrush, the redwing and many a touring Scandinavian opera-singer.

The blackcap's song is completely mad. Gilbert White called it 'a sweet, wild note'; *wild* is right – or rather, *wild* isn't the half of it. Cracked, drunken, loud, littered with chitters and whistles, and generally all over the shop – it doesn't sound at all like music to me, and I think that's sort of the point. The blackcap doesn't give a damn *what* it sounds like to me. Birds never do.

There's a gap, I think, between the noises the birds are making and the songs we're hearing. Birdsong belongs to the birds, but we've spent an awful lot of time trying to make it ours, too: we've translated it into poetry and crowbarred it into music; we've caged it and recorded it, copied it and studied it. We've transformed the way we hear it; we've even changed the way they sing it (and if we go on as we are we may end up silencing it – but that's something for the last chapter). In a thousand different ways, birdsong has inspired us.

Between the drumming tympanums of a bird's syrinx and the processing centres of the human brain, something fascinating is going on. It's been going on for thousands of years: us, the birds, their stupid language and what it says to us.

I

An Infinity
of Possibilities

Three lovely notes he whistled, too soft to be heard
If others sang; but others never sang
In the great beech-wood all that May and June.
– Edward Thomas, 'The Unknown Bird' (1915)

To the best of my knowledge, I've never heard a buck fart. But I *have* heard a cuckoo sing, if you can call it a song, so I have a rough idea of what the author of 'Sumer is Icumen in' had in mind. The song, also known as the Reading Rota,* is about the arrival of summer – so it's about a singing cuckoo, a farting buck, a starting bullock, calves and lambs, 'springing' wood-lands and sprouting seeds. It was written in the middle of the thirteenth century, and is the oldest known song of

---

* 'Reading' because the oldest manuscript copy was found at Reading Abbey in Wiltshire; 'Rota' because the song is a kind of part-song known as a rota or round (like 'London Bridge is Falling Down' or 'It's a Long Way to Tipperary').

its kind (that is, the oldest known polyphonic round) in English. In translation from the Wessex dialect, it begins:

> Summer is a-coming in
>
> Loudly sing cuckoo
>
> Groweth seed and bloweth mead
>
> and springs the wood anew
>
> Sing cuckoo!

Even back then – when Dafydd ap Llywelyn was rising up against the English in Wales, Roger Bacon was compiling his scientific masterpiece *Opus Majus* in Oxford and Paris, construction was beginning on the 'new' abbey at Westminster – the English were writing songs about the birds singing.

But it wasn't just us. At around the same time, for instance, the Persian-language poet Jalāl al-Dīn Rūmī was also celebrating birdsong: 'Birdsong brings relief / to my longing / I'm just as ecstatic as they are, / but with nothing to say!' And it all goes back a lot further than the 1200s: we find birdsong in the Bible – 'flowers appear on the earth; the time of the singing of birds is come, and the voice of the turtle[*] is heard in our land', says the

---

[*]   That's the turtle *dove*, by the way – not an unexpectedly musical terrapin.

Song of Solomon – and in the millennia-old poetry of the ancient world. This thing has deep roots.

Why? Why is poetry so noisy with birdsong?

Birdsong is a wonderfully malleable material. We can make of it what we like; it's putty for the poet. And like putty or paint or music or ink, it can be put to work as an artist's medium, as a means of expressing ourselves. What we hear in birdsong, in other words, is more often than not the resonant echo of our own feelings.

The end of the poem isn't the end of this process. Birdsong has shaped our poetry, yes – but poetry, in its turn, has shaped the way we listen to birdsong, and what we think it's saying to us.

I heard my first cuckoo in the early summer of 2016, at the RSPB Otmoor reserve, a little way north of Oxford (I heard my first turtle dove – like a sort of soft, woolly power-drill – there too, that same sunny day, almost as soon as I'd climbed out of the car; it was my first time birding south of the Peaks, and it felt as though Otmoor had parcelled up the lowland English pastoral tradition, just for me).

On hearing the cuckoo's call, I didn't exactly throw

back my head and cry *Lhude sing cuccu!*, but I'm sure I cracked a smile. It was a bright, warm day; I had a summer's morning to myself, and I'd just heard my first cuckoo; what was more, I would be attending the wedding of our dear friends Sam and Jeremy later on (that was why I found myself at such a dangerously southern latitude). I was, in short, happy – as was that thirteenth-century songwriter, as he anticipated the shortening of the shadows, the warming of the days, the greening of the land and the flatulence of the male deer.

But these things are subjective; how I felt on hearing that June cuckoo depended on me being me. Someone else might have felt something different. And had I been a dunnock – or a reed warbler, or a pied wagtail, or a meadow pipit – I wouldn't have heard anything in that lowing *cu-coo* but threat and menace.

Cuckoos are, of course, brood parasites. Cuckoo nestlings, born in the nests of other birds, destroy the eggs and young of those birds, and grow fat – we've all seen the picture, at once ludicrous and heartbreaking, of a tiny parent bird perched on the shoulder of a fledgling cuckoo five times its size, feeding it caterpillars – on their scarce and hard-won resources. Cuckoos visit horror on their hosts. *That's* what a dunnock or a warbler hears in the cuckoo's call.

It's a curious noise, the call of the cuckoo. It has a slightly hollow, woodwindish quality, suggestive of someone blowing across the top of a bottle; it's unhurried, almost complacent – pretty rare in birdsong – and low in pitch. I can, without too much effort, detect a note of languorous menace in it; if I were a breeding dunnock, I'm sure I would hear it loud and clear. And yet at the same time it does, as in the Reading Rota, have a meadowy, sun-steeped joyousness about it, too – it *is* the sound of sumer icumen in. The fact is, it's a cipher. What we find in it depends on us: on who we are, where we are, what day it is, perhaps even the books we read or the music we enjoy. It's as variable as the weather; it can shift with the orbit of the earth, and the changing of the seasons.

Consider the robin. The robin sings all year round, give or take a few embarrassed weeks of moulting in midsummer. Its music has long been well thought of: 'It is the opinion of some', wrote Nicholas Cox in 1674, 'that this little King of Birds for sweetness of Note comes not much short of the Nightingale.' The robin has, to my ear, a musical song – perhaps I think that because of the rather stately pauses the robin leaves between phrases, just like you hear in 'proper' music. You can hear robin-song in December as well as in May; there's some uncertainty, however, as to whether the song you hear is the same from one month to the next. Does the robin change the way it sings, or do we change the way we listen?

David Lack, author of the landmark 1943 study *The Life of the Robin*, states definitively that the 'autumn song', performed from September to late December, is 'thinner and less rich' than the 'spring song', which the robin uncorks around New Year and sings until mid-June.

Edward Grey, though, wasn't sure. Grey – properly 1st Viscount Grey of Fallodon – served as Foreign Secretary for nine years before the First World War. In 1927, towards the end of a life that had been busy with birdsong and much else, he published *The Charm of Birds*; it has hardly been out of print since. It's an idling and delightful book. Grey makes it clear right from the off that song is, if not the one thing that birds do best, then certainly the one thing that they do better than anyone else (except us, of course).

Of the robin's autumn song, Grey agrees with Lack that it has 'something thin and acid in its tone'. But he wonders if, hearing the robin amid the greys and browns of autumn, 'our own minds are attuned to a minor key, and we hear it in the robin's song'. Perhaps on a warm day in April, 'when sap is rising and we are full of anticipation, with ears a-tiptoe [*what* a turn of phrase] for the first note of a blackcap', we hear it differently.

'We used,' said a Conservative who was cutting my hair soon after the war, 'we used to think Mr Lloyd George was everything that was bad. Now we admire him. Is it he or is it we that have changed?' And so I ask, listening to a robin in spring and comparing the impression remembered of the autumn, 'Is it the song or is it I that have changed?'

Traditions in poetry and folklore can influence our perceptions of birdsong just as much as a wintry turn in the weather. Often, these traditions can persist for many generations. Sometimes, though, they break, or are broken; time-worn ways of thinking are flipped on their heads, and we find new ways of listening, and thinking, and feeling – we hear a new sort of music.

The work of one of England's most celebrated Romantic poets offers a good illustration of how this happens.

Samuel Taylor Coleridge's first nightingale poem, 'To the Nightingale', appeared in 1796. It's a work that seems to establish the poet in a direct line of literary nightingale-worship that ran back through Milton and

Sir Philip Sidney to the fourteenth-century poet Petrarch*
and beyond – into the ancient world, where the nightingale was said to be Philomel, daughter of an Athenian
king, raped and mutilated by her brother-in-law Tereus
and transformed by the gods into a bird (the Greeks
said it was a swallow, the Romans a nightingale). The
bird's song – Philomel's lament – pervades ancient literature: Sophocles wrote of the 'sweet, sojourning
nightingale', singing in the sacred grove; Aeschylus had
the prophetess Cassandra speak sadly of the 'shrill-voiced
nightingale'; the song of the musician Orpheus for his
lost wife Eurydice is compared by Virgil to 'the nightingale grieving in the poplar's shadows' (though in Virgil
the nightingale mourns not her own ordeal but the loss
of her chicks, stolen by a ploughman).

So impossibly sad was the nightingale's song to the
ears of these ancient listeners that it came to be believed
that the bird pressed its breast up against a thorn when
singing, so as to get an additional throb of anguish into
her music. Richard Barnfield, in Shakespeare's day, wrote

---

* 'That nightingale who weeps so sweetly, / perhaps for his
brood, or his dear companion, / fills the sky and country round
with sweetness / with so many piteous, bright notes' – from the
love-poem collection *Il Canzionere*, which Petrarch wrote over a
period of forty years, from 1327 onwards.

that the nightingale 'all forlorne, / Lean'd her Breast up-till a Thorne; / And there sung the doleful'st Ditty'.

Coleridge, in his 1796 poem, sticks dutifully with the same tradition: he addresses the bird as 'Philomel', and assumes that it is female (though female nightingales, unlike female robins, seldom sing); he even offers a quotation from Milton's *Il Penseroso*: 'most musical, most melancholy!' He heard the same sorrow in Philomel's song as all the other poets had – or perhaps he heard what he'd been told to hear.

Coleridge's second nightingale poem appeared in 1798, by which time he'd gone off that idea completely. Coleridge was a wildly curious poet, forever plunging – metaphorically speaking – into thickets in search of nightingales (he described himself as a 'library-cormorant', a wonderful allusion to the rakish seabird's reputation for diving deeply and devouring gluttonously). He knew his literary history, of course – but nightingales built from ink and sentiment weren't enough for him.

Coleridge's relationship with real-life nightingales is knotted up with his relationship with Dorothy Wordsworth. He'd fallen in with the Wordsworths – Dorothy and her older brother William – in the late 1790s. On one occasion, the essayist William Hazlitt described visiting the trio at Alfoxden in Dorset and finding 'Coleridge explaining the different notes of the nightingale to [Wordsworth's] sister' (scholars have suggested – pretty plausibly – that it was attentive, clever Dorothy who is more likely to have been doing the explaining, assuming that she could get a word in edgeways); later, in the spring of 1802, the pair went walking to nearby Stowey: 'Heard the nightingale; saw a glow-worm,' reports Dorothy's journal. Coleridge, with Dorothy's help, was learning a little more not only about nightingales but about nature.

In his 1798 poem, 'The Nightingale: A Conversational Poem', it's clear that Coleridge is seeing the world – and hearing the nightingales – differently. He bemoans the poets who spend all their time 'building up the rhyme' when they ought to be stretching their legs in the countryside and immersing themselves in the 'shapes and sounds and shifting elements' of wild nature (both specialities of the Wordsworths; few writers of the time can have been as robustly outdoorsy as Dorothy was).

He again deploys his Milton quote ('most musical, most melancholy bird!') but this time he's setting up Milton only to knock him down: 'In Nature there is nothing melancholy,' Coleridge insists. There's nothing mournful about the nightingale's song; we only think that there is because some unhappy 'night-wandering man' said so, and 'many a poet' – Coleridge is grinning here, knowing full well he was one of them – 'echoes the conceit'.

And so Coleridge kicks aside the shop-worn story of Philomel and reinvents the nightingale as 'the merry Nightingale / That crowds, and hurries, and precipitates / With fast thick warble his delicious notes' (it's a 'he', now, note). When he writes of 'a most gentle Maid' who dwells beside a grove of nightingales and 'knows all their notes' –

> And she hath watched
> Many a nightingale perch giddily
> On blossomy twig still swinging from the breeze,
> And to that motion tune his wanton song
> Like tipsy Joy that reels with tossing head.

– it's hard not to think that he's writing about Dorothy Wordsworth.

Nightingales didn't change between 1796 and 1798. Coleridge did. It would be too glib to say that 'To the Nightingale' is about the nightingales he'd read about in books and 'The Nightingale' is about the nightingales he'd heard in the woods, but there's definitely a tension here between the literary tradition and what Coleridge feels when – perhaps walking with the Wordsworths in the wooded foothills of the Quantocks – he hears a nightingale begin to sing.

This isn't about Coleridge being right and everyone else being wrong; it isn't that those earlier poets were insincere, or weren't listening properly. There *is* a note of tragedy in the nightingale's song, for those who are inclined to hear it. But there's joy, too, in the very same music, the very same phrases.

That wretched night-wandering man, Coleridge says, 'filled all things with himself, / And made all gentle sounds tell back the tale / Of his own sorrow'.

The sounds of birds tell us back our own tales.

In Nature there is nothing melancholy, Coleridge decided, in the end. This is a familiar idea for us: the natural world as a thing of perfect beauty, as unspoilt, ideal, something to which humankind should aspire. It's an idea that took some heavy hits in the Victorian age – think of Darwin and the 'wasteful, blundering low & horridly cruel works of nature', or Tennyson's 'Nature, red in tooth and claw' – but it's still with us, recognisable and influential.

Back then, though, it was radical. Nature, before the Romantics, was for most people a thing to resist – a thing that could starve you, freeze or flood you, kill your livestock, plunder your crops, infest your home. Civilisation was salvation; nature was the enemy.

The Romantics – William Blake, John Clare, the Wordsworths, Keats and Coleridge among them – changed that. The Romantics were on nature's side. When you think about what 'civilisation' looked like at the start of the nineteenth century – the filth and noise of industry, the misery of the city slums, the sufferings of the urban poor – it's not hard to see why. Nature was a sanctuary from all that: an asylum for over-worked, over-stressed, over-civilised man. Looking at the world this way transformed not only what we saw in nature, but what we heard in it, too. Not least among the achievements of the Romantics was the extent to which they reinvented birdsong.

The best known of all English skylark poems is 'To a Skylark' (1820),* by another Romantic, Percy Bysshe Shelley. On the page, the poem has something of the

---

* George Meredith's 'The Lark Ascending', from sixty years later, might score higher on name recognition, but that's largely down to Ralph Vaughan Williams' 1914 musical interpretation of the same name, with its quivering soprano violin-lark.

shape of a lark's flight: tall, wavering, sometimes halting but unbroken to the end (the display-flight, in case you're not familiar with it, is a fluttering climb into the blue, shivery and near-vertical, like a ping-pong ball being carried upwards on an intermittent stream of air; the lark can keep it up for as long as an hour, and may reach a height of 300 metres). Flight, of course, has a lot in common with birdsong: they both, in their different ways, put the birds beyond us, out of our reach; they both speak to us of escape and freedom, and they both, throughout history, have made us long to emulate the birds, and live as they live – or rather, as we like to think they live.

But Shelley's poem is more about the song than the flight. And it's not about what the lark is saying; it's about what Shelley is hearing: a 'flood of rapture', a 'happy strain', 'shrill delight', 'unpremeditated art'. Addressing his lark, Shelley declares that 'Shadow of annoyance / Never came near thee' (nonsense, from an ornithological perspective: male skylarks are extremely tetchy in the singing season, and will fly fiercely at intruders on their turf); by contrast, *our* songs, human songs, are always compromised by melancholy ('Our sweetest songs are those that tell of saddest thought'). The lark, in its flight and song, embodies for Shelley something divine, something painfully and impossibly beyond our reach. Shelley longs for uncomplicated happiness, and so he hears it in the skylark's song.

Skylarks aren't divine, of course, or anything like it. They have muscles and blood and skulls and lungs and hard-beating little hearts; they live in a fast muddle of fear and rage and lust and, maybe, joy, too, of a sort. They're not really all that different from us. But that's a hard thing for a Romantic poet to take.

We can pin down Shelley's skylark, incidentally, with some precision. It wasn't, it turns out, an English lark; it was Italian, and its song staked out a territory among the myrtle hedges of Livorno, in the west of Tuscany. His poem was born during an evening stroll with his wife, Mary, in the summer of 1820. The bird's song broke free of the landscape, taking the poet's fancy with it.*

Landscape is about continuity; change, if it comes, does so slowly – or, if it comes quickly (a forest burns, a sudden storm breaks, a river bursts its banks), the change is

---

* In his poem 'Shelley's Skylark', written in Livorno, Thomas Hardy mourns the 'little ball of feather and bone' that 'moved a poet to prophecies'.

an event. You could say that birdsong, for us, is an event of this sort: part of the landscape, but at the same time able to transform it, and give it new meaning. Sometimes birdsong feels like a bright pin stuck in a map. *Look*, it says – *look here.*

A singing skylark rising from a meadow or moor in twittering display-flight brings this metaphor to life. The flight and song jut upwards from the land, making, for a short time, an eminence, a sort of fleeting monument – or perhaps, if you tilt the landscape through ninety degrees, a hook on which to hang a poem.

In poetry, birdsong is more often than not an event; birdsong is the thing that leaps up at us out of a landscape.

Imagine a bright, freezing morning on a heathland hill, one day in January. There are a few small birds about: linnets in the sedge-grass, hungry goldfinch squadrons roving from alder to alder. You've had a slurp from your flask of tea (no sugar, so it tastes rotten, but at least it's hot) and now you're kneeling in a puddle, fumbling in your pocket for a ring, and about to ask the person you love to marry you. Can you imagine it? Congratulations: you are now me, not so very long ago. It's quite a moment – a moment that stands apart, stands out from the flatlands of our ordinary days (and don't worry: she says yes).

Now we'll depart from how it really was. Imagine that, in this moment, a bird begins to sing. A blackbird's burble ringing out over the bracken and heather bents. A late robin striking up its bright modulations from its perch on the trig-point (specifically, trig point TP0971, Baildon Hill). An improbable nightingale singing in key with the light aircraft buzzing by overhead.*

You'd remember it, wouldn't you? It'd be different from other bird songs that you'd heard on other days. It would be an event. It would be special because of the moment in which it occurred, in which you heard it – but the moment, too, would be made more special by the fact that the bird sang.

In Thomas Hardy's 'The Darkling Thrush', the poet encounters 'An aged thrush, frail, gaunt, and small, / In blast-beruffled plume' singing a 'full-hearted evensong' in the growing gloom of a winter's night. Hardy describes the 'land's sharp features' as resembling 'the century's corpse outleant', and so the historical setting is clear – we're at the dog-end of the nineteenth century, with the twentieth hoving heavily into view.

---

* In reality, I don't think any birds sang. I like to think that there were skylarks overhead. I don't really mind whether or not there really were.

Hardy, being Hardy, sees 'little call for carolings' in the barren winterscape (and by implication in the century to come), but the song of the thrush – his 'happy good-night air' – gives the poet a faint hope that things might not be so bad, after all; that the thrush might know something he doesn't.

It all reminds me of a famous picture by the Kearton brothers, early pioneers of both photography and birdsong recording: their 'Primroses Photographed in the First Moments of the Twentieth Century' is really just a workaday picture of some flowers; throw in the human context, though – the time on the clock, and the day on the calendar – and it becomes a thought-provoking work of art.

Hardy, similarly, has to tell us that the old century is dead – and that the frost was spectre-grey, the ancient pulse of germ and birth shrunken hard and dry, and all the rest of it – to give meaning to the thrush's joyful song. It's not quite the same as Edward Grey being 'attuned to a minor key', and hearing it in birdsong; Hardy hears minor keys all around him – in the orchestral setting, so to speak – but the thrush's riffing solo is a counterpoint, a contradiction to the darkness: a contradiction, in fact, to the landscape.

This is an interplay of influences, of subtle shifts in interpretation between the bird, the place, the time and the human listener. And then, of course, poetry adds a further dimension: Hardy writes his poem, and we read it, and – in a small way, but still – we'll never listen to a thrush's song in quite the same way again.

There's more to the poetry of birdsong than skylarks and nightingales. Ted Hughes exalts the diminutive, punchy, rattling wren; the Dorset dialect poet William Barnes declares that the blackbird 'do zing the gayest zong'; Robert Frost hears the tit-like ovenbird ('a mid-summer and a mid-wood bird') singing in the lull of July.

Every era has its own angles on birdsong, every society its own priorities and preoccupations – and every poet, of course, brings to the subject their own freight of experience, language, insight and emotion.

In the nineteenth century, Emily Dickinson listened to the song of an orchard oriole (or possibly a Baltimore oriole) and concluded that the significance of the song was in the ear of the beholder –

> The fashion of the ear
> Attireth that it hear
> In dun or fair.

– while the Massachusetts poet John Ciardi, meditating on a mockingbird, came to a double conclusion: that birds have nothing to say, but that not to listen to their songs is 'the death of rapture'. For Ciardi, birdsong is meaningful not because of what the bird is trying to get across but because of what he, waking to its noise on a summer's morning in Florida, is reminded of on hearing it.

There's no one way to listen to birdsong; there are no rules for its interpretation, no code for translating a twitter or a *tsee-tsee* or a *jug-jug-jug* into poetry. Perhaps that's why our poets return to it again and again, saying something new, something different, every time.

Let's look at one more nightingale: John Keats's nightingale, which – according to a disputed account by Keats's friend Charles Armitage Brown – was heard by the poet from 'a grass-plot under a plum-tree' at Wentworth Place (now Keats House) in Hampstead, north London,* in the spring of 1819. The resulting ode is one of the most famous poems in English.

For Keats – who was just twenty-three at the time – the nightingale's song *was* a constant, a single, unvarying song, a golden thread connecting him with the far-off past: 'The

---

* The chances of hearing a nightingale in Hampstead today are roughly similar to those of hearing one in Berkeley Square, as in the 1939 song by Eric Maschwitz and by Manning Sherwin.

voice I hear this passing night was heard / In ancient days by emperor and clown'. He makes an aching equivalence of the call of the bird with the call of home, imagining that the Old Testament heroine Ruth might have heard the same poignant nightingale's song when toiling homesick in the barley-fields of Judah, 'amid the alien corn'.* It's an alluring idea: when the world is a whirl, when everything around you seems to be moving at a gallop, a bird's song reminds you that some things stay the same – that a nightingale still says *jug-jug-jug*, that spring, when it comes, will bring with it the noises of swift and swallow, chiffchaff and blackcap – that you really *can* go home again. You can pretend that birdsong is a fixed point in a changing world; you can forget, for the duration of a blackbird's evensong, that change is what nature *does* – that change, development, dynamism, is really the whole point of living things.

Illusions of this sort can be powerful. Keats, in the 'Ode to a Nightingale', isn't just listening to the bird's song; he's overwhelmed by it. It hits him like a drug: 'as though of hemlock I had drunk, / Or emptied some dull opiate to the drains'. Keats, in this poem, is essentially drunk on birdsong.

---

* Technical note: it's pretty unlikely that she did, because, although nightingales do breed in the Southern Levant – roughly equivalent to the land of Judah – they wouldn't be singing much at harvest-time.

The biologist Richard Dawkins, in his book *Unweaving the Rainbow*, takes Keats's account at face value, and considers his symptoms from a neurological perspective. The song, he argues, acts like a narcotic on Keats because to all intents and purposes it *is* a narcotic. Nightingale song has been refined over millennia in the chem labs of evolution to have an uproarious effect on the nervous systems of other nightingales – to set a complex cocktail of hormones and neurotransmitters fizzing into life in the nightingale brain. Keats, Dawkins admits, 'was not a nightingale' (fair point, Prof), but he *was* a warm-blooded vertebrate, and a distant cousin to the nightingale; most drugs that work on one vertebrate will have a similar effect on others, so it's not unreasonable to think of the bird's song as a drug.

A recent biography of John Keats caused something of a stir by claiming that the poet spent the spring of 1819 – a fertile period that also produced the 'Ode to Indolence' and 'La Belle Dame Sans Merci' – in the numbing grip of opium addiction. According to Dawkins' reading, Keats was certainly a poet under the influence that spring, but his narcotic of choice was the product not of the poppy but of the nightingale.

Is this why it means so much to us? Is birdsong really zipping across the gaping eons of evolution that separate us from the birds – around 310 million years, give or take – and booting up the same neuro-chemical responses that make male birds want to fight and female birds want to settle down and start a family? I'm not sure we can ever really know for sure. Consciousness is complicated; neurobiology is never as simple as those '10 Ways to Boost Your Serotonin!' magazine features like to make out. But it may well be a part of the picture.

When you look at it this way, it seems possible that the appreciation of birdsong is hardwired into us, literally a part of our DNA, of who we are. Our poetry is a process of looking at who we are – how we work, what we feel, how we respond to the world we move through – and playing with it, exploring it, testing its strengths and its limits. So it was inevitable that birdsong would find its way into our poems, and that, in doing so, it would take many forms, be many things.

'I contain multitudes,' declared the American poet Walt Whitman, finding room within himself for contradiction, contrast, multiplicity. The same is true of us all: we are unfathomably complicated things. Perhaps this is why birdsong – a spectrum of many colours, or, better, a chord composed of many notes – seems to speak to us. It, too, contains multitudes. There's an infinity of possibilities in birdsong.

2

A Song of Many Parts

'To improve my stock of metaphors.'

– Samuel Taylor Coleridge,
when asked why he attended
lectures on science

Harry Mortimer Batten knew how to cut a Romantic down to size:

> O Cuckoo! shall I call thee Bird,
> Or but a wandering Voice?

That's Wordsworth, of course – lines three and four of his 1802 poem 'To the Cuckoo'. The poem is part of the eleven-stanza *Ode: Intimations of Immortality from Recollections of Early Childhood*, in which the poet (then a hoary thirty-two years of age) reflected on the loss of innocence and man's connection with the divine in nature. In 'To the Cuckoo', the bird's 'twofold shout' recalls to Wordsworth the 'golden time' of his schooldays; then, as now, he writes, the cuckoo was 'No bird, but an invisible thing, / A voice, a mystery':

> To seek thee did I often rove
> Through woods and on the green;
> And thou wert still a hope, a love;
> Still longed for, never seen.

H. Mortimer Batten, author of *Our Garden Birds* (1934) and numerous other popular nature works, wasn't having any of it. 'How Wordsworth can have lived in the Lake District and yet from his schooldays till middle manhood have known the cuckoo only "as a wandering voice" is surely beyond the intelligent observation of the present day,' he wrote. 'Wordsworth must have seen thousands of cuckoos. Probably he thought they were sparrowhawks or something.'

But then, as Batten points out, 'it was only recently that it was realised that poetry might be used to express common sense, and it is as well not to take the word of bygone poets with regard to natural history subjects'.

It's an exercise in advanced point-missing, of course. Batten is being wilfully obtuse. Cuckoos *are* elusive, more easily heard than seen (if not literally invisible), and so Wordsworth uses the bird and its shout as a metaphor for those other things that we can sense but not see, whose calls we can hear but which remain out of sight and out of reach – transient happiness, glimpsed spirituality, fleeting enlightenment. But try explaining that to H. Mortimer Batten.

This has long been a fraught relationship. Appropriately enough, it has to do with territory. At the first sign of an interloping poet on his patch, the ornithologist is up on his perch, fluffing his plumage and clearing his throat: 'Now it's all very well saying "the lark's on the wing", Mr Browning, but what *species* of the family Alaudidae are you referring to, exactly?' And the poets are often no better, because can birdsong *really* be just a question of hormonal balance and molecular genetics, is beauty something you can log on a sonogram, aren't the ornithologists missing the whole *point*? . . .

The fact is that there's poetry in the science and science in the poetry; each needn't be a lone cock-robin, chippy and turf-fixated, scrapping on the borderlines for each fraction of territory. There's plenty of common ground.

Look, for instance, at *this* character: an expert, a man who clearly knows his bird songs inside out, jibing at 'outsiders' who are less well informed:

Your Londoners . . . I believe fancy every bird they hear after sunset a nightingale. I remember when I was there last walking with a friend in the fields of Shacklewell we saw a gentleman & lady listning very attentive by the side of a shrubbery and when we came up we heard them lavishing praises on the beautiful song of the nightingale which happend to be a thrush.

So, in the 1820s, wrote John Clare, the Northamptonshire labourer's boy who was perhaps England's greatest nature poet – a poet, yes, but an expert too, and as protective of his hard-earned knowhow as any university don. (Clare knew his 'clod-brown' nightingales and their 'out-sobbing songs' well. His poem 'The Progress of Rhyme' offers a careful transcription of the bird's 'witching notes': 'Chew-chew . . . cheer-cheer . . . cheer-up cheer-up cheer-up . . . tweet tweet jug jug jug . . . wew-wew wew-wew, chur-chur chur-chur, woo-it woo-it, tee-rew tee-rew tee-rew tee-rew, chew-rit chew-rit . . . will-will will-will, grig-grig grig-grig'.)

Let's consider two ways of looking at a nightingale.

One is that *Luscinia megarhynchos* is an insectivorous passerine species of the family Turdidae (or perhaps Muscicapidae), migratory between the Afrotropical and

Palearctic realms, divisible into races *L. m. megarhyn-chos*, *L. m. africana* and *L. m. golzii*. Its song is varied and unstructured, with abrupt pitch changes and a sudden, throaty trill.

The other is Shakespeare's 'lamenting Philomel', the grieving songstress of Virgil and Ovid, Aeschylus and Sophocles; the bird's song is a high requiem, a plaintive anthem, choral minstrelsy, a wanton song, the voice of desire, a throe of the heart, a mournful melody of song; it expresseth what grief her breast oppresseth.

I could go on, at length, in either vein. What *is* a nightingale? It's both and neither of these things. It's 21 grams of blood, muscle, feather and bone. To call it a species is to fit it to a framework that no nightingale would comprehend, a human framework; to talk about the status of a species – whether it declines, whether it thrives – is to tell a story that, to a nightingale, would make no sense at all. These are human ideas, structures we've put together for our own purposes (even if that purpose is to protect nightingales; a nightingale, really, is too busy to give a fig whether we protect nightingales or not).

The scientists and the poets have essentially been doing the same thing all this time. They've constructed a nightingale. They've built the thing we now associate with the word 'nightingale', and it's not the scientists' idea of a nightingale, or the poets', but everyone's: it's the *human* idea of a nightingale, and it really is a terrific thing. It's a thesis and a poem and a moodboard and a spider-diagram and a song and a symphony – and it's all still embodied, just about, in that lurking, flitting, tail-pumping handful of feathers, hollering in a Sussex hazel thicket and trying not to die.

In practice, we each of us only get to see the nightingale we've built from a certain angle, and at a certain distance; none of us ever sees the whole thing. But from what we see of it, we each build our *own* nightingale, and carry it about with us – and I think that's pretty terrific, too.*

When I think of a nightingale, the stuff from the poetry side and the stuff from the science side aren't kept apart: the whole lot bundles together into a busy jostle of nightingale-ness (Coleridge out-shouting the rest, but years of bird-book study in there too [rufous rump, pale eye-ring, breeds May–Jun, 5–7 eggs], along with scraps of T. S. Eliot and the memory of the only

---

* Andrew Whitehouse, curator of the 'Listening to Birds' website that I mentioned in the Prologue, prefaces the site's 'nightingales' with the splendid comment: 'In some cases these might not have been "real nightingales" but maybe that depends on what you think a "real nightingale" is.'

living nightingale I ever saw: an unlikely vagrant outside
my halls-of-residence window one autumn day in York).
They don't mix, exactly – the same way I'm still me and
you're still you if we're thrown together in a crowd – but
I can, so to speak, hear them both at once, just like you
can hear two duetting streams of song from a songbird's
double-barrelled syrinx.

The American poet Amy Clampitt wrote a wonderful
poem called 'Syrinx'. In it, she compares the syrinx* –
the bird's voice box – to a 'foghorn that's all lung'. It's a
wind instrument, too imprecise to shape consonants; the
soaring song, in the end, is 'pure vowel'. Clampitt finds
freedom – freedom from detail, from 'the particular' –
in birdsong. But this isn't the ethereal music of a 'blithe
spirit'; this is no 'wandering voice'. Birdsong here is a
material thing, a fact of bioacoustics and the physics of
air; Clampitt draws a clear line from the properties of
the syrinx – its limitations, in fact – to the qualities of
the song.

---

* Pronounced 'sirrinks', not 'sy-rinks'.

This is why I'm here in a gloomy lab in the bowels of Leeds University's Garstang Building, poking about in a partridge.

This book isn't just about birdsong; it's about the places where birdsong and human culture overlap and interact. It's easy to forget that science is a culture, too.

'The trachea bifurcates here, into two primary bronchi,' explains Dr Peter Tickle, tweezering apart the tissues, 'so you've basically got a dual voice-box; air can pass over two vibrating surfaces. So it can sing two different notes at once.' Peter is a research fellow in the university's School of Biological Sciences, and he's kindly agreed to show me what a syrinx looks like.

In Seamus Heaney's poem 'Widgeon', a man plucking a widgeon (a kind of wild duck, larger than a teal but smaller than a mallard) finds the bird's 'voice box'. He blows on it, and finds himself making 'unexpectedly / his own small widgeon cries'.

It might be a poem about the appropriation, the theft, of voices that aren't our own. Or it might be about keeping alive a voice that has fallen silent. But it *is* unexpected, in any case; that *this* – a hollow nub of gristle, no bigger than a broad bean and filmed with sticky blood – can make *that*: a widgeon's yelping whistle, or a partridge's cluck, or a cuckoo's diphone, or a blackcap's wild note

– and from there, a Coleridge poem or a Messiaen flute piece or simply that kick of the heart that greets the first chiffchaff song of the summer. It all stems from a modified half-inch of windpipe.

'Unexpected', in fact, barely covers it. It seems miraculous.

After the dissection, Peter shows me some videos made by researchers of birds' syrinxes* in action – and these, too, seem miraculous. Look them up on YouTube (search for 'universal mechanisms of sound production'). They're amazing. The slowed-down monochrome fluctuations of the membranes of the syrinx in full (simulated) song are alien and extraordinary and madly beautiful. There is, again, nothing ethereal here; we can see ribs of cartilage, glistening expanses of translucent membrane – everything you don't want to find in your chicken sandwich. But then the air ripples through and the muscles (here triggered by electrodes) contract; what the researchers call 'tissue waves' flutter through the syrinx, over and over. It becomes gulping and squid-like. And this is the thing that makes the song.

Some people might think that it spoils or devalues birdsong, looking at it in this manner, breaking it down

---

* Pedants will tell you that the correct plural is 'syringes'. Ignore them.

into its component parts. I'd disagree. Birdsong acts on us, as we've seen, in a lot of different ways: it can accentuate our happiness, or pile melancholy on top of melancholy – and (another thing we've learned from the poets) it makes us want to talk about birdsong. Meanwhile, we learn from the scientists that – like anything that's unusual, and beautiful, and complex, and mysterious – birdsong also makes us want to *learn* about birdsong.

The syrinx is the *how* of birdsong. We'll talk about the *where* in the next chapter – which leaves us with the *why* and the *what*.

Why do birds sing?

This is a very old question. Poets, as we have seen, have tended to take the anthropomorphic view: they sing, as we do, to express exultation (in the case of the skylark, for instance) or despair (in the case of the nightingale).

Ornithologists prefer to find reasons in nature, in the evolutionary history of the species. Singing must have benefits – must, that is, give the bird a better chance of producing offspring, and passing on its genes down the family line – so what we have to do to nail the *why* is figure out what those benefits might be.

Whole books have been written on this. David Rothenberg's wonderful *Why Birds Sing* runs to 288 fascinating pages. Charles Hartshorne's landmark 1973 work

Born to Sing has 304.* For our purposes, though, a list will
do. Birds call and sing:

1. To attract a mate. A song thrush's song is an *OK
Cupid* profile pinned to the top of a tree.

2. To say what sex you are. In species where there isn't
much difference between males and females – where,
to use the jargon, there's little sexual dimorphism –
there's a tendency for songs to be correspondingly
more complex.

3. To establish and maintain a territory. This is an
important one. Singing is very often a safer alternative
to fighting with rivals ('war minus the shooting', as
Orwell said of sport).

4. To indicate that you're ready to breed.

5. To maintain a pair-bond. I take my wife a cup of
tea every morning; a female song sparrow sings to
its mate. Same principle.

---

* This, too, is a book worth looking up. There's much to enjoy in
Hartshorne's blithe certainty that the beauty of a song can be scien-
tifically measured: one diagram shows a scale running from 'beautiful'
to 'hopelessly superficial', while Hartshorne's all-time worldwide
'Best 194 Songbirds' list is full of interest (the superb lyrebird tops
the chart with a score of 999.669:48).

6. To signal changes in your domestic arrangements – whose turn it is to incubate the eggs, for instance.

7. To let your offspring know where, who and what you are. This often begins while the young are still in the egg. It works the other way round, too: the superb fairy wren of Australia teaches its young a 'password' song while they are still in the egg; should a cuckoo lay in a fairy wren's nest, the new-born cuckoo won't know the 'password' and will be rejected by the mother.

8. To make it clear what species you belong to (or what population of a species).

9. To hold your flock together. The honking of geese in their sky-wide skeins and the *seep* of red-wings migrating at night are 'contact calls' designed to ensure that no one goes astray.

10. To intimidate enemies. Often doesn't work.

11. To warn others that there's a predator in the vicinity. Think of a blackbird's runaway *chupchup-CHUPCHUP* or the blue tit's rising rattlesnake *churr*.

12. To practise. To sing well, you have to put in the hours. 'How do you get to Carnegie Hall?' asks the

old joke. 'Practise!' Same here, but substitute 'How do you get to perpetuate your genetic material?'

Do birds ever sing because they're happy? That really depends on what you mean by 'happy'. Charles Hartshorne suggests that 'animals find their chief pleasure in their essential activities'. All that means, really, is that birds like being birds. I can go along with that, I think. Put it this way: it's not that they sing because they're happy, and it's not even that singing *makes* them happy – I think that perhaps the singing *is* the happiness, and the happiness is the singing. Which might mean something or nothing.

This, anyway, is a relatively modern conversation to be having. In the earliest days of ornithology we never gave much thought to the *why* of the natural world, because we were always too busy figuring out the *what*.

For much of our history as a species, we learned about birds because we lived among them. Knowing about nature was how we stayed alive. Which birds were good to eat? How could we catch them? Where could we find birds' eggs? Could birds' calls warn us about danger? Sometimes the information we gleaned from birds was even more arcane: the Borana Oromo people of northern Kenya, for instance, learned to find the nests of wild honeybees by studying the movements of a songbird known as the honeyguide.

This model stayed pretty much the same for a good while. Asking 'why' wasn't really a part of natural history. Birds just did what they did; they'd simply been made that way. If they sounded happy, then they *were* happy, like characters in a children's story. Or perhaps they sang to please us – it was for us, after all, that the world had been created.

And, for most of human history, our attempts to answer the question of *why* songbirds sing have tended to circle back, one way or another, to happiness. And we're not just talking about the proto-naturalists of the ancient world here, or even just the fowlers, bird-catchers and 'natural philosophers' of the Middle Ages. As late as 1836, a scholarly article in *The Magazine of Natural History* eventually resorts to the conclusion that spring weather (a blue sky, balmy air, 'a lovely fragrance wafted by gentle zephyrs') is all it takes – 'all is admirably calculated to infuse delight into the mind' – and so the birds, thus delighted, start to sing, like a carefree gentleman as he takes off his socks, rolls up his trouser cuffs and settles himself in his deckchair on the first day of his summer holidays. It's not, to say the least, a very scientific reading of the facts; it gives us an idea of how little progress had been made by that point in the field of bird behaviour.

There were one or two exceptions (there generally are). Gilbert White, the all-seeing parson of Selborne, was one: he and his correspondent Daines Barrington agreed (correctly) that birds sing more through rivalry with other males than in an attempt to 'charm' females. In the early nineteenth century, George Montagu, a forensically observant soldier-turned-country gent who, after White, has the best claim to be the founding father of British ornithology,* concluded (also correctly) that singing males were not trying to seduce but to advertise – less a serenade, more a yell of 'Come and get it'. 'Their business in the spring', he wrote, 'is to perch on some conspicuous spot breathing out their full and amorous notes, which, by instinct, the female knows, and repairs to the spot to choose her mate.'

---

* Montagu ID'd the first 'Montagu's harrier' – a bird of prey that breeds in our fens and fields and winters in the scrub of the Sahel – in the summer of 1803. He also established that the bird known as a 'Greenwich sandpiper' was in fact only a ruff in winter plumage, while the 'ash-coloured sandpiper' was actually a knot.

A rock-pooler as well as a birdwatcher, he is commemorated not only by Montagu's harrier but by Montagu's blenny, Montagu's ray, Montagu's sucker and Montagu's sea snail.

Not too long afterwards, of course, Darwin and *The Origin of Species* came along; 'why?' stopped being a pointless question to ask about birds, and started being an incredibly complicated one. After Darwin, it became clear that seeking the causes of birds' behaviour – and of everyone else's behaviour, come to that – would carry us deep into evolutionary history. Eventually, the question evolved to become a whole field of study: ethology. From the 1930s onwards, ethologists like Niko Tinbergen and Konrad Lorenz began to fill in some of the detail on 'why', and we began to understand birdsong not simply as an avian version of 'tra-la-la' or 'zip-a-dee-doodah' but as a code and a language, in which birds spoke of fear, rivalry, anger, lust and family. And perhaps happiness, too, who knows.

That leaves us with the 'what'.

What is birdsong? What, exactly, specifically, does a blackbird sound like? We know it when we hear it, of course – but then it's gone, dissolved in sky and lost for ever. Birdsong is a wildly unstable element; it has a shorter half-life than carbon-10. If we want to study it – and of course we do, because we're only human, and curiosity, no less than wonder, is one of our weaknesses – we need to freeze it.

It's notoriously difficult to describe birdsong with any sort of consistency. In the early part of the twentieth century, ornithologists devised various methods of transcription, of getting the eccentric music of songbirds down on paper.

In the US, Aretas A. Saunders was an early pioneer. Saunders was an obsessive data-gatherer, a compulsive observer of birds (and plants, and insects, and mammals). He wasn't just a box-ticker; he didn't just want to know, say, what song a Swainson's warbler sings – he also needed to understand how the bird and its song fitted in with all the other birds, bird songs, insects and animals that shared its habitat.

In 1915, Saunders presented a new technique whereby a song could be mapped on x and y axes according to its pitch, duration and intensity (a fourth variable, sound quality, by which he presumably meant tone or *timbre*, was considered 'baffling and difficult to describe with accuracy', and so was left out). It was a ramshackle approach that relied on a good ear for music (the y axis was simply the GABCDEF musical scale). Saunders himself was aware of its limitations – he described the complicated process of determining a song's intensity as 'destined to try to the utmost the patience and perseverance of the future student of bird song' – but defended himself by popping open a philosophical can of worms: 'Can a bird song be described accurately and exactly? No, nor can anything else.'

That's true, up to a point: there are always levels of detail, depths of zoom, that our methods are inadequate to describe. But still, it was possible to look at one of Saunders' charts and think '*surely* we can do better than this'.

The debate that followed – conducted largely in the pages of such august organs as *The Auk*, the journal of the American Ornithologists' Union – was vigorous, learned and ultimately doomed. In 1931, the future of birdsong study came rumbling into view on the back of a flatbed truck.

Stewart Park in the city of Ithaca, NY, was once the indigenous village of Neodakheat; since then, it has been Military Lot 88, a school athletics venue and a film studio (silent-moviemakers Ted and Leo Wharton set numerous three-reel melodramas against the park's wild backdrops); in the mid-twentieth century it had a funfair, carousel, zoo, vaudeville theatre and all. The park still sprawls over forty acres of land beside the glacial Cayuga Lake. Stand in the park in late spring with your ears open, and you've a good chance of hearing palm warbler (*tsink*), house wren (*dirrd*), northern waterthrush (*spwik*), blackpoll warbler (*tzzz*), rose-breasted grosbeak (*peek*), yellow-rumped warbler (*see-seet-seet-seet-seet-trrrr*), blue-grey gnatcatcher (*pwee*), song sparrow (*sweet*), warbling vireo (*git, vidervidi*), and white-crowned sparrow (*pink*).

It was these birds – or their far-off forefathers – that, in 1929, made history.

Arthur Augustus Allen – known as 'Doc' – was the first professor of ornithology in the United States. He was a storyteller, a writer, a lecturer and a teacher as well as a scientist. He'd discovered fifteen new tropical bird species before his thirtieth birthday. In 1924, he found a family of ivory-billed woodpeckers – widely feared extinct* – nesting in Florida. Another ornithologist, James Tanner, wrote that 'all the ivory-bills that I have ever seen I located first by hearing them call and then going to them', so it seems likely that Allen, too, was alerted to the bird's presence by its call (a nasal, tooting *kent*, sometimes likened to a child's tin trumpet) – all the more so as Allen had a phenomenal ear for birdsong.

---

* And today, sadly, almost certainly extinct: despite a flurry of excitement over some possible sightings in Arkansas and Florida in 2005, the American Birding Association classifies the bird as 'definitely or probably extinct'.

But it was becoming obvious that the human ear – even one as refined as Allen's – was no longer adequate as a tool for the scientific study of birdsong. One way or another, we had to figure out how to *preserve* birdsong – to set it down in a permanent record.

So in the spring of 1929, Allen and his team at Cornell University set up camp in Stewart Park.* Using modified motion-picture gear from the Fox Movietone studio, carried on the back of a flatbed, they recorded the house wren, rose-breasted grosbeak and song sparrow (to recap, that's a *dirrd*, a *peek* and a *sweet*) on synchronised movie and audio film. This, remember, was only two years after the release of Al Jolson's *The Jazz Singer*, the first full-length motion picture to use synchronised sound – and in the same park where Lionel Barrymore and Irene Castle had hammed it up for the Wharton brothers' silent three-reelers. These recordings formed the basis of Cornell's Macaulay Library, which is now home to more than 175,000 individual recordings of birds, mammals and insects. Allen would surely have been staggered – and delighted.

---

* Allen's team was soon joined by another major figure in the history of recording, Albert R. Brand, notable for having made a fortune on Wall Street before the age of thirty and bailing out to work with Allen just months before the Crash of 1929.

'He was dedicated to educating the public and I think he'd be thrilled with the outreach that's possible today,' Macaulay Library archive audio curator Greg Budney commented on the 100th anniversary of that day in Stewart Park. 'With the click of a mouse, anyone can access sounds in the archive. From locations ranging from a field in the Midwestern US to deep within the Amazon basin, to the Himalayas, the Macaulay Library offers a fantastic window into nature, open to everyone.'

Allen's weren't, though, the first recordings ever made of bird vocalisations. After all, sound recording had been around since 1857 (when Édouard-Léon Scott de Martinville created a 'phonautograph' that translated sounds into patterns scratched in soot). In 1877, Thomas Edison's phonograph cylinder introduced the concept of playback, not only recording but *recreating* the sounds it heard. I can't imagine how magical that must have seemed (no matter how crackly, or lo-fi, or indistinct the sounds) – and I can't imagine how joyful the eight-year-old Ludwig Koch must have felt when, on returning home from a trip to Frankfurt Zoo in 1889, he played back the wax-cylinder recording he had made on his Edison machine – a gift from his father. What he would have heard, muffled, oddly distant and softened by static, was the song of a white-rumped shama, an

Indian songbird related to the flycatchers and prized for its thrush-like song. In south Asia, shamas are often kept as cage birds; here, spilling from the brass trumpet of the Edison Home Phonograph, was an abstracted version of the same thing – birdsong in the drawing room, automated and on demand. Little Ludwig's shama-song was the first ever recording of a singing bird.

The technology advanced, as technology does; milestone followed milestone. Cherry Kearton recorded the first wild birds – a song thrush and a nightingale – on an Edison at Kenley, in the green belt south of Croydon, in 1900; another nightingale was 'bagged' by Karl Reich in Berlin, and released as the first gramophone record of a singing bird in 1910; an emperor penguin – not known for its song, but capable of a resonant and far-carrying kazoo effect – was recorded via radio transmission in 1934; the first stereophonic birdsong record, Sten Wahlström and Sven Åberg's *Birds in Stereo*, hit the shelves in 1963 (the idea of buying birdsong on LP doesn't seem so quaint when you consider the vast popularity of Radio 4's daily 'Tweet of the Day' birdsong broadcasts).

Recorded birdsong, though, has the same problem as live birdsong. You can't put it in a book or a scientific paper. You can't study it in a library reading room. You can't corral it into graphs, charts and scales. Even on vinyl or magnetic tape, it's wild and unwieldy. To study bird-song properly – to really get into its workings, and figure out all its moving parts – we needed to get birdsong down on paper. With all due respect to A. A. Saunders and his x and y axes, though, there still wasn't a strictly objective way of translating the songs the scientists could hear into something they could see.

Fortunately, the government was working on it.

There's a lot in the history of birdsong science that feels odd and incongruous. Those tiny electrode-controlled syrinxes, singing and dancing for the cameras; the heavy rig of early Hollywood shipped into a public park to grab a snatch of wren-song. Strangest of all, though, is the cutting-edge knowhow of the US military-industrial complex being put to use in recording a robin's song.

During the Second World War, code-breaking was a life-and-death priority for Allied military intelligence. Coded comms often made use of shifts in sound frequency and timing; a technology that could analyse these kinds of patterns would give the Allies a vital edge. Bell Telephone Laboratories was put on the case.

Working in the shadows, Bell – a firm with its origins in the earliest days of telecoms technology, and by this point something of a genius factory – began to develop devices designed for 'the visual translation of sound'. The military applications of these devices went beyond code-breaking; accurate analysis of sound signatures could also be used to ID the propellers of ships and planes.

As early as 1943, though, this top-secret technology was already being put to non-military uses. Bell's 'sound spectrograph' or 'sonagraph' was made available as a tool for helping the deaf to recognise sounds – when answering the phone, for example, or listening to the wireless – and to learn to speak. The researchers were also, it seems, alert to the potential of the sonagraph in studying birdsong; a 1944 paper from Bell Labs featured 'sonograms' not only of human speech but of the calls of the northern cardinal, northern mockingbird, brown thrasher, eastern screech-owl and American robin.

Sonograms, the author of the paper wrote, would make it possible to 'analyze, compare, and classify the songs of birds, and, of even more importance . . . to write about such studies with meaningful sound pictures that should enable others to understand the results'. This was birdsong, translated – and not into the pentameter of poetry, but into a language scientists could understand.

I'm looking at a sonogram of a blackcap song right

now; it was recorded in Ryedale, North Yorkshire, last summer, and I found it on the xeno-canto song-recording website.* It's a graph, essentially – it's not a million miles away from A. A. Saunders' version, except that the y axis shows not musical notes but frequency, measured in kilohertz. The data, the meat of the graph, is quite different, though: where Saunders drew tidy lines, the sonogram is a canvas of smudges, grey on white, as if someone had taken a soft-leaded pencil and wiped it sidelong over the page.

It has, like those quivering syrinxes, an unusual sort of beauty. It looks like something from the last days of Impressionist painting – but that's misleading, because there's nothing impressionistic about it: this is hard data, clear-cut, for all its apparent smudginess. What looks like a faded thumbprint on the chart is a lode of technical information. Just as a trained musician can 'read' the notes in a musical score – perhaps hearing the music in her head as she goes along – an expert in bioacoustics can look at a sonogram and see birdsong. The important difference is that a musical score is an instruction, a

---

* www.xeno-canto.org. At the time of writing, xeno-canto has 3,622 different recordings of blackcap songs and calls. If you wanted, you could spend just over forty-three hours and fifty minutes listening to blackcaps.

representation of what *should* be; a sonogram is a recording – it shows you what *is*.

Or what was. Once, years ago, I was taken to a fancy restaurant where, as an after-dinner gimmick, the waiter offered each of us a choice of cognacs from the year of our birth. Thanks to xeno-canto, I can give myself a similar sort of treat now. I sort the library of blackcap recordings by date, scroll back through the decades – and I'm in luck. 1978. April, 1978, five months before I was born, but near enough. It was recorded by a man called Patrik Åberg in Illmitz, Austria – a national park, up against the Hungarian border. The sonogram looks much like the others: a parade of rippling ink-smudges, spiking up and down between 3 and 15 kilohertz. It looks like a collection of pale-grey feathers laid out on a sheet of paper. I play the recording, and it's perfect. It's as exuberant and eccentric a blackcap as I ever heard, breathless, reckless, full of squeaks and raspberries, roller-coastering through the frequencies. It's nice to know that thirty-nine years ago, in the year I fell into the world – the year of three Popes, of the first test-tube baby, of *Superman* in the cinemas; the year Ian Botham hit 108 and took 8–34 in a single innings against Pakistan; the year of *Parallel Lines* and *All Mod Cons* and *Darkness on the Edge of Town* – well, it's nice to know that blackcaps then sounded like blackcaps now. It doesn't mean much, but it's nice anyway.

'*That* was a *chack*,' Graham says, pointing at a holly-bush on our left. '*That*' – now he jabs his finger at a young elder by the stream, on our right – 'was a *tack*.'

We're in woodland to the north of Leeds, in the valley between the suburbs of Gledhow and Chapel Allerton. It's mid-afternoon, and it's November; birdsong-wise, this is the dead zone, but here we are anyway. I met Graham Shortt to talk about birdsong – specifically, about Graham's remarkable ear for birdsong – and it seemed silly, despite the season and the drizzle, not to at least try to put him to the test.

I had heard from local birders that Graham was a 'whiz' at ID-ing birds by their songs and calls. Over email, he concedes that his abilities probably place him in the top 0.3 per cent of UK birdwatchers (actually he puts it more modestly than that: 'Somewhere in the top 1,000,' he says, but I run the numbers later). We meet for a drink in his local. I want to talk to Graham because I want to know how it works: how it's possible to find a note in a fog of ambient noise and think – no, *know*

– 'that's a treecreeper' or 'that's a bullfinch' or whatever it might be. I've seen it done many times, and it looks like witchcraft to me.*

He's a big man, Graham, tall and wide, maybe five or six years older than me (I'm always happier when experts are older than me) – he's easy to spot when he walks into the pub. We take a table in a corner, and I ask him to tell me the story of his birding life. He's articulate and philosophical; he has a decent sense of proportion about his obsessive streak, and, it quickly becomes clear, a frighteningly comprehensive knowledge of birds.

In between birding anecdotes ('Brett Richards[†] once picked up a snow bunting from three miles out') and idiosyncratic tips on bird ID ('You've read *Of Mice and Men*? The golden plover is George, the grey plover is Lenny'), Graham gives me an expert's-eye-view – or ear-view, I suppose – of the world of birdsong.

'Most people have the idea that bird songs are stereotypes,' he says. 'But you have to learn the *voice*.' It's not

---

* Sometimes it makes me feel like my great-uncle Frank, who, in the days of the 'Magic Eye' puzzle craze, flatly refused to believe that people were seeing what they said they were seeing, and concluded that we were all simply making it up.

† Legendary east-coast twitcher who admits to having scheduled his wedding in March 'because it's the worst month for birding and I was least likely to have to postpone the event'.

about the notes and rhythm, he argues; it's all about tone. That's right – the elusive property that the keen-eared A. A. Saunders found 'baffling and difficult to describe'. So that's helpful.

This approach puts Graham at odds with the received wisdom. Take the songs of the garden warbler and black-cap, for example: two wayward babbles, often said to be very much alike. 'They're *nothing* like each other,' Graham says, in a tone of exasperation. One 'bubbles', he says, and the other 'flutes'. But then he has difficulties of his own: the sedge warbler and reed warbler aren't often singled out as 'problem' species in terms of song ID (the reed warbler's is 'more even, less varied and lower pitched', according to my guidebook*), but for Graham they're tough to tell apart.

He tells me that he learned his birdsong studiously, by rote, from CDs he played in the car (he reckons that he clocked over a thousand miles in his first six months of serious birding). For all that, his seems to be a hugely personal way of responding to birdsong. It's about getting to know the birds – and not only the birds, but the landscapes in which they live. The *where* and *when* of

---

* Gilbert White, incidentally, thought that the sedge warbler was 'a splendid fellow': if he could be 'persuaded not to sing in such a hurry', he wrote, 'he would be an elegant songster'.

birdsong can be as important as the *what*; stripped of context, Graham says, some songs can be near imposs-ible to identify.

The *chack* and the *tack*, by the way, were a wren and a robin. I'd noticed that, in the autumn, robins start breaking out the wren impersonations, tutting – *chack*-ing – very like wrens. No no no, Graham said; they're quite different. I'm afraid I forget, now, which one went *chack* and which one went *tack*.

Also in the woods, as we passed a small lake pitted by raindrops and peopled with idling white gulls, Graham was sure he heard a Mediterranean gull yelp amid the general chatter of their black-headed cousins. Later, I'll listen to recordings of the two species online; I can hear the difference (the Med gull's is higher-pitched, and more abrupt; the black-headed gull emits a strangulated seagull yell – there's a reason why the black-headed gull in *Watership Down* was called Kehaar), but the idea of me ID-ing the two by ear in the field – over the noise of the weather, the other birds, our conversation and the monotone of the traffic on the nearby Gledhow Valley Road – is laughable.

For an expert like Graham, I realise, a bird's song or call is as much a part of the bird's identity as its appear-ance, while ID-ing that song is itself tied into multiple observations – perhaps made only half-consciously – about the season, the location, the landscape and a good deal else.

Earlier, Graham had quoted a friend who described birdwatching as 'a heuristic and compass to the natural world'. Listening to birdsong is the same. It's a means of orientation; it's embedded in habitat, landscape and place.

Before we part, Graham tells me another birdsong story.

He was birding in Gambia, he says – that riverine strip of west Africa, surrounded by Senegal and the sea. It's well known as a birder's paradise; a trip with a knowledgeable guide might yield bearded barbet, beautiful sunbird, bronze mannikin, blue-breasted kingfisher and sundry other tempting exotica.

It was here that Graham heard a birdsong he remembers more fondly than any other: 'a perfect descending scale', coming from a treetop. It was a willow warbler, in Africa on migration. They're ten-a-penny in England between March and August.

'It was like meeting an old friend,' Graham says. Like, I suppose, coming home.

3

Coming Home

'However strangers sound such words,
That's how we sound them here.'
—Thomas Hardy, 'The Spring Call' (1909)

We were in one of the Paris railway stations, I
forget which one – it was sprawling, grey and
complicated, too many people, not enough places to sit
– Gare du Nord, Gare Montparnasse? I don't remember.
But I *do* remember the sparrows.

While my wife fetched coffee I sat on my suitcase
and watched them busy beneath a line of metal benches.
A sparse, grubby shingle of pastry flakes, Metro
tickets and cigarette ends had accumulated there. City
sparrows are used to having to find their calories in
unpromising places. These were mostly hens, *Parisiennes*,
grey-to-brown and undistinguished; a good fit for the
concrete and dull steel of Gare du whatever-it-was.
They made me wonder how long it had been since I'd
seen English sparrows behaving like this: mucky and

bustling, streetwise and on the scrounge. They made me think of home.

House-sparrow numbers in Britain have fallen catastrophically during my lifetime.* No one's sure why: it might be disease or air pollution, it might be predation by cats or sparrowhawks, it might be that they have nowhere to nest, it might be any combination of these factors. Nowadays, they aren't exactly uncommon – you'll often experience them as a vast noise of chirruping, a Commons debate wound up in pitch to a half-dozen kilohertz, coming from inside a beech hedge – but when I was a boy in the West Yorkshire suburbs, perhaps twenty-five years ago, they were more than common, they were *everywhere*. They maintained a knockabout mob rule over our bird table and got up to all sorts in our guttering; in the streets and shopping precincts, they scavenged and scrapped and begged and generally did exactly what these French sparrows (*piafs*, as they're known) were doing in the railway station.

---

* I later learned that the *piafs* of Paris suffered a population crash, too. The city cherishes its raffish sparrows, and yet – for no obvious reason – numbers fell by around 200,000 over a seventeen-year period. One French newspaper argued that home improvements in ramshackle housing districts had deprived the sparrows of cosy homes in broken roofs, flawed guttering and tumbledown walls, and called the sparrows 'victims of gentrification'.

Watching the sparrows made me think of home, but what home, exactly? England? Wakefield? My mum and dad's 1970s semi in leafy WF4? And just as important as 'where' was 'when'. As I sat on my suitcase on that Paris platform, en route to northern Spain, was I thinking of the England I'd just left behind, or was I thinking of the past (a quite different foreign country, as L. P. Hartley wrote, where the sparrows, just as much as us, do things differently)?

From Paris Gare du Nord – leaving the sparrows behind – you can take a train due north, to Amiens or Abbeville, and in barely more than an hour find yourself deep in the green countryside of Picardy and Arras and French Flanders. This is a landscape of wounds. A century ago, these were the killing fields of the First World War; the Western Front, a wavering stripe of brutally broken land, ran south-east across northern France from the coast of Belgium to the Swiss border. Countless men – at least four million – died here. Now, it's a land of memorials (Thiepval, Vimy, Loos, Villers-Bretonneux, Neuve-Chapelle) and cemeteries (Étaples, Vermelles, Thiaucourt-Regniéville, Pheasant Wood).

It's also now, as it was then, a land of beech woodland, hedgerow and cultivated pasture – what further west they call *bocage* – which means that it's a land of birdsong.

'It has often seemed to me that gunfire makes birds sing,' wrote Stuart Cloete, who served for four years on the Western Front. 'Or is it just that the paradox is so great that one never forgets it and always associates the two?'

To English soldiers far from home – and I can only imagine how desperately, hopelessly far the 140-odd miles between Flanders and Dover must have seemed to the young men at the Front – there was a particular poignancy to the birdsong of the battlefield.

'Every morning when I was in the front-line trenches I used to hear the larks singing soon after we stood-to about dawn,' wrote Major F. H. Keeling. 'But those wretched larks made me more sad than anything else out here. Their songs are so closely associated in my mind with peaceful summer days in gardens or pleasant landscapes in Blighty.'

The pastures might have been torn apart by trench-work and shell-fire – what the geographer Joseph Hupy called 'bombturbation' – but the skylarks remained.

So too, in the shattered woodlands, did the nightingales. In his landmark cultural study of the war, *The Great War and Modern Memory*, Paul Fussell noted that 'Flanders and Picardy abounded in the two species long the property of symbolic literary pastoral – larks and nightingales.

The one now became associated with stand-to at dawn, the other with stand-to at evening. (Sometimes it is really hard to shake off the conviction that this war has been written by someone.)'

There isn't anything especially English about these species. England sits right on the north-western brink of the nightingale's natural range (even the nightingales that do come here treat us a summer time-share, and spend seven months of the year at their African wintering grounds). You might hear the song of a skylark (or, rather, a *Feldlerche*) in the chalk grasslands of Germany's Rhineland or on the plains of Extremadura (where it's an *alondra*). In one sense, there was no reason why the 'wretched larks' of the Western Front should have made poor Major Keeling ache for Blighty. Of course, sounds, like smells and flavours, can be powerfully evocative (if I sniff the glossy solvent-smelling pages of my first birdwatcher's field guide, I'm eight years old again); of course, a poignant Proustian rush can strike any of us at any time, often from the most unexpected quarters. But why the skylarks *in particular* – any more than, say, a cumulus cloud or a blade of grass or the taste of fresh bread?

It's a fair guess that Keeling had read about Shelley's 'blithe spirit', his 'high-born maiden in a palace-tower' and her 'music sweet as love' (never mind that Shelley's was an Italian skylark); we can suppose that he'd read Meredith hymning the 'simple singing of delight, shrill, irreflective, unrestrain'd', or maybe Christina Rossetti recalling 'one sunny morn' when 'the earth was green, the sky was blue' and she saw and heard 'a skylark hang between the two, a singing speck above the corn'. It seems less likely that he would have read, or in any case remembered, the German poet J. W. von Goethe's 'when aimless skylarks jubilate above us in the spacious blue' or Joseph von Eichendorff's 'Just two skylarks upwards soar, day-dreaming in the scent'.

Shelley and Meredith and Rossetti and the rest had planted an English flag in the skylark's song. You didn't have to be a raving jingo – indeed Keeling, a well-to-do socialist who rejected the frothing anti-Germanism of some of his contemporaries, was certainly no such thing – to hear something English in the sound of the bird.

There's a disconnect – a gulf, sometimes – between what we *think* is British and what is actually, physically, geographically British. This applies as much in birdsong as anywhere else.

In reality, there is only one quintessentially British bird song. It's a trilling, high-pitched twitter that you might hear coming from the canopy of a pine forest in Highland Scotland; it's the song of the Scottish crossbill, *Loxia scotica*, and it's a song you'll hear nowhere else in the world.

The Scottish crossbill is a burly forest finch with a twisted beak strikingly adapted for prising seeds out of pine cones. It's Britain's only endemic bird species – that is, the only species unique to us. But to say so is to open up a taxonomic can of worms.

Not so long ago, the red grouse, *Lagopus lagopus scotica*, was considered endemic to the UK. It's a bird that perhaps more than any other has shaped our country (quite literally: acres of heather moorland have been tailored – cropped, burnt, fenced off and deforested – to suit the grouse, or rather to suit the people who like to shoot the grouse). Its look – red wattle, plumage rich as fruitcake, furry white spats – is iconic, and so is its sound: the grouse's throaty cluck, calling *go back, go back, go back* across the black peat and heather bents, is one of the keynote voices of our upland biophony.

But the taxonomists – the biologists whose job it is to identify, label, and sort life on earth into manageable hierarchies of phylum, order, genus, species and so on – took the red grouse away from us. Our grouse, it turned out, was really not much different from *their* grouse; the 'willow grouse' or 'willow ptarmigan' of North America, China, Russia and most of Europe was, taxonomically speaking, pretty much the same bird as our red grouse; our bird was not a species in its own right, but only a subspecies. That same spine-tingling *go back* clatter can be heard across the better part of the northern hemisphere.

Taxonomists, however, are even-handed tyrants, who giveth just as well as they taketh away. In August 2006, the Scottish crossbill, previously lumped in with the far more widely travelled common or red crossbill, was declared a species – an endemic British species.* What differentiated *Loxia scotica* from *Loxia curvirostra* (or for that matter the bulkier parrot crossbill, *Loxia pytyopsittacus*)? It was partly the bird's physiology, and partly its manner of flight – but most of all, it was the Scottish crossbill's call. *Loxia scotica* speaks with a Scottish accent.

Mind you, it takes a well-trained ear, an ornithological Henry Higgins, to hear the difference. Comparing

---

* The British Ornithologists' Union had actually conferred 'species' status on the Scottish crossbill way back in 1980, but their evidence hadn't been enough to sway the RSPB.

recordings of the two species' 'excitement calls' I found online, I'd say that the Scottish crossbill's repeated *chup, chup* has a lower pitch and mellower tone than that of its common cousin (later, I'm pleased to find that the RSPB's ID guide agrees with me, contrasting the ' "chup chup" call with a fluty quality' of *scotica* with the 'loud "chip chip" call' of *curvirostra* and the ' "kop-kop" and "choop choop"' calls of *pytyopsittacus*). But is all this really enough to make *scotica* a species apart? I say 'grass' with a flat 'a' and pronounce 'scone' to rhyme with 'bone' – am I a different species to my friend Ben, who is from Suffolk and says 'grarse' and 'scon'? RSPB studies found that, although there were no notable genetic differences between Scotland's *scotica* and *curvirostra*, the birds maintained independent populations – that is, individuals of one type never bred with individuals of the other. But then, Ben and I have never interbred either.

The divergent forks you see in taxonomic charts – where the vertebrates went *this* way and the invertebrates went *that* way, or whatever – always seem so decisive. In reality, speciation is a muddy and confounding business.

Our sole endemic species is a dapper little finch, and I wish it all the best, but even the Scottish crossbill's most ardent admirers would have to admit that the bird isn't packing much in the way of star quality. I don't feel a surge of teary patriotism when I examine the sono-grams of *scotica*'s excitement call. The Scottish crossbill is uniquely Highland, uniquely Scottish, and uniquely British – it has carved a niche deep in one of our ancient landscapes, but it doesn't *feel* more Scottish than, say, the osprey (a summer migrant from Africa) or more British than the red grouse (common as muck from Alaska to Archangelsk). This seems very unfair on the Scottish crossbill.

Biology – the collected happenstances of birth, breeding and evolution – isn't enough. Publicity is what counts. Think of it as a PR campaign: with Keats and Coleridge manning the nightingale hype-machine and Meredith, Rossetti and Vaughan Williams puffing the sky-lark for all they were worth, how could these birds and their songs fail to make an impression on our national cultural consciousness? Notions of Britishness have sel-dom made much sense; they don't *have* to make much sense to make an impact. We've never really cared about how foreign our British kings and queens have been – and as a rule they've been more foreign than not – so why would it be different for nightingales?

Britishness is whatever you want it to be. Sparrows chittering in the gutters. Swifts, just in from the Congo, screaming thinly through the twilight. The twanging, high-pitched *pyah* of an Indian peacock on the lawn.

In northern England, a chaffinch is sometimes called a 'spink'. In the Midlands, it can be a 'pie finch'; in Scotland it goes by 'shielyfaw' or 'shilfy' or 'britchie'; the Cornish called it an 'apple bird', and in Northumberland it might be a 'shavey'.

But these things work both ways. Chaffinches have dialects of their own.

When I was young, and the house sparrow was king, there weren't many chaffinches to be seen round our way. When one did turn up, in and among the beige-and-grey blitzes of sparrows, it was distinguished by more than its white double wing-bar; a chaffinch – even a female, dressed for comfort in buffs and browns – has the bearing of an aristocrat. Its forehead is high and its beak – the grey of very soft pencil-lead – has a neat, just-sharpened point; the male's call of *spink* is peremptory. I liked chaffinches. But I never noticed their song.

As with so many things in life, I read about it before I got round to experiencing it for myself. I'd picked up a book about the polar explorer Edward Wilson in a second-hand bookshop somewhere. Wilson, who died with Captain Scott on their return journey from the South Pole in 1912, was a gifted artist and a distinguished ornithologist (when he perished in Antarctica he was midway through a major study of disease in British grouse). His wildlife illustrations drew on more than a keen eye for visual detail; rather, he sought to depict 'the idea of an animal': 'When one knows the animal well enough – little bits from years and years ago when one first saw the animal in a hedgerow – it's all there ready to come to hand when at last you say, now I am going to paint it.' There's no doubt that, for Wilson, songs and calls were bundled with form, colour, character and habitat in his conception of a bird's identity. He saw birds in all their dimensions; he painted, in the deepest, richest sense, from life.

Diaries from Wilson's youth in the countryside outside Cheltenham include a series of mnemonics for recognising the songs of the local birds: *just a wee little bit* is the blue tit, *easy, easy, ease a bit, easily with it a bit* the treecreeper; a starling goes *kiou, kiou, kiou-kiou, kiou, kiou, kiokio, kiokio* – 'like the jackdaw – then 3 single blackbird's notes, full mellow and contented; then a long dribbling rattle with its beak'. I can't help wondering if Wilson replayed these songs to himself as he slogged across songless Antarctica, a decade later; I wonder if he ever heard in his head the note of the grouse: *go back, go back.*

This, anyway, was where I first read that the chaffinch's song has the cadence of a fast bowler in cricket running up to the crease and delivering the ball.

It probably wasn't Wilson's invention; the chances are that he lifted it from the popular nature writer William Warde Fowler (who noted further that on some occasions, early in the singing season, the chaffinch seems rusty: he is liable to get to the wicket and stop, and takes a few days of practice to 'deliver the ball'). It caught my attention, in any case. I'd always known that there are few things in life that can't be improved by a clever cricketing analogy; if anything could help me get a hand to the flashing top-edged half-chance that birdsong seemed to me to be, cricket could.

Chaffinches start singing as early as February (well before the beginning of the cricket season). My family rented a holiday cottage in Hawkshead, near Windermere, one April. By that time the local chaffinches had settled into their groove and were singing incessantly* in the

---

* According to Mark Cocker, co-author with Richard Mabey of *Birds Britannica* (Chatto & Windus, 2005), a cock-chaffinch in its singing prime will repeat its principal phrase about six times a minute, and up to 3,000 times a day. The record for the most balls bowled by one

Lakeland pines and birches. I listened for the sound of the fast bowler – and, to my surprise, I heard it. The accelerating run to the wicket, pacey and staccato (it's a short run, around eight paces – Pakistan legend Wasim Akram bowled off about the same); a little flourish or convolution of notes as the bowler gathers in the ball and enters his delivery stride; then *pew*, the brief whistle of the ball flying from the bowler's hand.

Just like that, I could recognise a chaffinch's song – or, to be more precise, I could recognise a *Cumbrian* chaffinch's song.

It's long been believed that chaffinches in different parts of the country sing their songs a little differently. In the days of bird-catching (which we'll talk more about in Chapter 5), skilled catchers were supposed to be able to tell a Kent chaffinch from an Essex chaffinch by slight variations in their song's final phrase: in Essex, the birds sang *chuckwado*, while on the opposite bank of the Thames, in Kent, it was *kiss-me-dear*.

But this was just the tip of the iceberg. In the early 1950s, English botany graduate student Peter Marler was surveying potential nature-reserve sites in Scotland when he realised that the songs of the chaffinches around him

bowler in a single day's Test cricket, by contrast, is 288 (C. F. Root, Old Trafford, 1926).

were changing as he travelled from valley to valley. He observed the same thing in the Lake District, while taking mud samples (perhaps he heard the forefathers of my Hawkshead chaffinches). His next job took him to the Azores, an archipelago some 350 miles off the coast of Portugal; in fact, he wangled the job mainly because he knew there were chaffinches there, and these, too, had their own song variations.

Working in his spare time, Marler – who would go on to be a monumental figure in the field of birdsong study – compiled the first 'dialect maps' for chaffinches (or indeed for any songbird). Intriguingly, the findings suggested that the songs a chaffinch sings aren't genetically hardwired, any more than that flat 'a' of mine is determined by my DNA; rather, a young chaffinch learns its songs from its father.

The comparisons with human dialect break down, however, because chaffinch song is *even more varied* than human speech. A 1982 study of chaffinches in Orkney, Sussex and Cheshire concluded that the variations within a geographical area were as great as the variations between different areas; it was not possible, the researchers found, to distinguish between Orkney, Sussex and Cheshire chaffinches as readily as you might tell a Scottish accent from an English one. There are two reasons for this. One is that young chaffinches aren't flawless recording machines; they'll often learn a song imperfectly, bodging their father's phrases, which means that the song – like many an old ballad – is warped and altered as it passes down the family line. The other is that chaffinches move about: a bird that learns a song in one location will very likely wind up singing it in another. (Actually, something similar happens in human accents: the great linguist David Crystal once told me that, far from making the way we speak more homogeneous, our modern tendency to drift away from our home towns has created *more* variation; it's just a lot harder now than it once was to identify an individual accent. 'It's very difficult now to do a Henry Higgins,' he said.) Even the most intensively diversified English dialects – think, perhaps, of the highly local 'Pitmatic' dialects once spoken in the close-knit mining villages of the north-east, where the difference between one dialect and another might be a matter of a mere half-mile – can't compete with our chaffinches where variation is concerned.

But there are birds that maintain clear-cut local dialects. One, the white-crowned sparrow, is native to the US (Peter Marler called it 'the chaffinch of the west'). Another, however, is a familiar sight here in the UK. The redwing, *Turdus iliacus*, is a favourite species of mine, and a regular on my local patch, but I've never heard one sing. That's because they only come to us in the winter, and save their songs for the woodlands of Norway and Sweden – their 'home', if ever a migratory bird can be said to have a home.

The redwing in Britain is a handsome character, neat and compact with a clotted-cream eyestripe and rust-red flanks, but it can cut a rather sorry figure when the frost begins to bite. It arrives from the far north in October, knackered and hungry; you'll often hear its faintly hoarse contact-call of *seep, seep, seep* from high overhead (for any birder, it's a long-awaited sign that autumn, season of migration, movement, vagrants and rarities, is finally under way). It fills up on berries and, when the berries are all gone, takes to the fields in busy, worm-hunting working-parties of perhaps fifty or sixty birds. The redwing is nordically indifferent to cold, but once the cotoneaster and rowans have been stripped it needs soft soil in order to feed; hard frosts in the late winter spell starvation. One nature writer of the last century wrote that 'a Redwing starved to death used to be no unfrequent sight in the course of a winter's ramble'.

It's easy for us in Britain to see the redwing's life as a desperate and wintry one, and to think of this dapper little thrush as a rather sad creature of bleak field and black hawthorn. Far better to follow the redwing back (in imagination or otherwise), in late spring, to its native forests; there, the identity of the redwing – not just as a species, but as an individual bird, of this copse in Krokskogen, or that beech wood in Moldemarka – is tightly bound up with its song.

I've listened to a recording of a redwing singing. It's a nice noise, uncomplicated, twittery and sharply resonant. But I haven't heard it belted out by a springtime cock-redwing from the top of a Scandinavian aspen – the Victorian naturalist W. C. Hewitson described it as 'perched upon the summit of the highest trees, pouring forth its delightfully wild note' – which means, really, that I haven't heard it at all.

And I've only heard one redwing dialect. In Norway alone, there are thousands.

The researchers Tron and Tore Bjerke studied redwing songs in the woodlands north of Oslo in the 1980s. They found that the birds' dialects differed distinctly – enough to be heard by the human ear – according to which territory the birds sang in; a new dialect could be heard around every sixth kilometre (Norway covers almost $400km^2$ in total, and most of it is home to breeding redwings). What's more, the boundaries between territories were sharply delineated (the Bjerkes found that redwings singing close to a territorial boundary would occasionally drop into the neighbouring dialect, but that the songs remained distinct: there was no hybridisation, no redwing equivalent of 'Franglais' or 'Hinglish'). Song territories persisted from one breeding season to the next, meaning that redwings returning from their wintering grounds to the south were able to find their way home with startling accuracy.

Why do redwing dialects maintain their integrity, while chaffinch dialects splinter? The main reason is that the redwing sings, as a rule, only one song; a chaffinch might sing as many as six, which provides much more scope for confusion and variation.

A Scandinavian forest full of redwings, each devotedly singing his father's simple song: this is where birdsong and place truly interconnect. It seems a bit silly – no, it *is* a bit silly – to use concepts of home, family, identity and culture when you're talking about a thrush, but it's also silly to think that skylark vocalisations have anything to do with a nation-state, and we do it anyway. We can't help it, it seems. These kinds of concepts – flawed, limited and human – are often, like the words of the languages we speak, the only tools we have for making sense of the world.

Rupert Marshall, a researcher at Aberystwyth

University, has made a study of local 'dialects' in another British species, the corn bunting. It's an increasingly scarce farmland songbird, with the look of a streaky, beefed-up sparrow and a jangling, jittery high-pitched song (Dr Marshall, who may have gone somewhat native in the course of his studies, prefers to describe it as 'like dribbling silver, a warm babbling brook on a sunny day, a soft, gentle trinkling – a joy to behold'; I can't agree, but I'll give the doctor bonus points for 'trinkling').

Marshall writes on his project's website that bunting dialects differ over a very small distance. ('Rather than thinking of Liverpool and Manchester, think of one side of a street compared with the other.') In places where the corn bunting has declined – that is, pretty much every-where except for a handful of Scottish islands – the dialects have lost their definition or vanished altogether, resulting in what Marshall calls 'a general mish-mash of songs'. For him, a corn bunting's dialect is part of its identity as a species: 'If we succeed in saving corn bun-tings but they no longer exhibit the behaviour for which they were once so well known' – if they no longer sing in dialect – 'can we truly say we have saved them? Imagine a lion that no longer roared.'

Birdsong in poetry, as we've seen, is often presented as a contrast to a landscape – as an event, rather than something stitched into the backcloth. In reality, it doesn't normally work that way; in reality, birdsong normally isn't the headline, isn't the lead story. For most of us, most of the time, birdsong is context.

I'm not a poet. I write fiction; I tell stories, and that means that – on a small, scruffy and distinctly un-godlike scale – I build worlds. World-building, counterintuitively, is about the little things. It's about the power of cumulative detail, rather than the star-power of stand-out showstoppers; it's about odds and ends being built up and up and up into something rich and complex.* I like scope and scale and sweep and all those sorts of things. Maybe this reinforces my feeling that nature – hell, that *life* – is about the ensemble cast, rather than the A-lister; the orchestra, rather than the rock star.

---

* My wife, who is much cleverer than me (but couldn't tell a chiffchaff from a willow warbler if her life depended on it), works in complexity science, so I just asked her to clarify the difference between 'complex' and 'complicated'. She said that if you can predict what's going to come out by looking at what's going in, it might be complicated; if you know what's going in but still can't say what's going to come out, that's complexity.

In a novel, birdsong is usually background; used skilfully, though – like a minimalist musical score – it can furnish context, texture, mood and a built-in, organic sense of place.

Thomas Hardy, whose darkling thrush feels like the bird at the centre of the world, also knew how to knit birdsong into the sprawling patterns of a novel. His 1892 tragedy *Tess of the D'Urbervilles* tells the story of the country girl Tess Durbeyfield. Tess's journey – I won't spoil the plot, but I can tell you it doesn't end well – is soundtracked by shifting tides of birdsong. Sometimes they signal that life – nature, England, the Wessex countryside, locked into its time-worn ways – goes on ('the birds shook themselves in the hedges, arose, and twittered'); they can echo and amplify Tess's happiness ('in every bird's note there seemed to lurk a joy') or her despondency ('only a solitary cracked-voiced reed sparrow greeted her from the bushes by the river, in a sad, machine-made tone'); at the moment of her downfall, the birds are silent in the trees overhead, roosting 'in their last nap'.

The birds, in many ways, are incidental; barely there traces in the currents of the novel. In other ways, though, they are vital – they, along with a thousand other details, act like drawstrings, pulling the novel together, fastening Tess and Angel Clare and Alec D'Urberville more tightly into the mesh of place, time and plot. This is birdsong as landscape.

We don't often notice background noise in fiction, perhaps because writers don't think about it much, either. Only a few spring to mind: there's the clangour of the bells of medieval Paris in Victor Hugo's *The Hunchback of Notre Dame*; there's the 'rough music' of Londoners shovelling snow from their doorsteps in Dickens' *A Christmas Carol*. But Hardy wasn't alone among nineteenth-century novelists in using birdsong to add an additional dimension to his landscapes (and his tragedies).

George Eliot's 1859 novel *Adam Bede* has themes in common with *Tess* – one reviewer at the time objected to Eliot's insistence on 'the startling horrors of rustic reality', foreshadowing the moralist uproar that broke around Hardy's novel thirty-odd years later – and shares, too, an intimacy with the noises of the English countryside.

Eliot was a novelist with an ear as well as an eye: at daybreak in Hayslope, 'daylight quenches the candles and the birds begin to sing'; Adam Bede, walking in winter, hears 'the gurgling of the full brooklet hurrying down the hill, and the faint twittering of the early birds'; the touches and glances of the early days of a love affair are compared to 'the first-detected signs of coming spring ... though they be but a faint indescribable something in the air and in the song of the birds'.

It's not that these are especially vivid descriptions of birdsong (both Hardy and Eliot, you'll have noticed, fall back on the catch-all 'twittering'); it's just that they're *there*, intrinsic to the worlds that Adam Bede and Tess Durbeyfield inhabit. And they inhabit them more fully because the birds are singing in the hedgerows.

But novelists aren't the only ones to have realised the transformative power of birdsong as backdrop.

'We use sound effects to paint pictures that stretch beyond the frame,' says Helen Dickson, 'and birdsong is no exception.' Helen is a sound editor whose work has been heard on television, film and radio productions ranging from week-night detective dramas to versions of *Macbeth* and *Under Milk Wood*. There's more to birdsong on film, she tells me, than the obvious – crows in a graveyard, say, or an owl hooting over a night-time establishing shot. Springtime song can be deployed to create a relaxing effect; conversely, the noises of birds of prey – the *scraa* of a peregrine, perhaps, or a red kite's *peee-oww* – can lend a note of anxiety or menace (their tone often comes across as 'mocking', Helen says). A well-timed peacock's shriek can lighten an atmosphere like a funny one-liner.

Birdsong is particular useful because of its many-layered associations with time and place. Screaming swifts – as heard in the BBC's 2016 *War and Peace* production – tell you, without making a big deal about it, that we're in the northern summertime. Geese honking overhead suggest that the year has turned, and that winter is coming. The jabber of roosting starlings might place us in a city at dusk as effectively as the glow of neon or the hire light of a cruising taxicab. These are noises that do their work – take us to other places, at other times – without us really noticing.

And if you want to convey a sense of unease, of things not being quite as they ought to be, birdsong can be tinkered with: slowed down, or played backwards, or lowered in pitch (the calls of baby owls and swans were manipulated to create some of the dinosaur noises in *Jurassic Park* – but that's another story).

It's easy to get it wrong.

'Placing birdsong is a delicate art,' Helen says. 'It can easily be overdone. We don't want the viewer to be removed from the moment. Repetitive sounds and too many effects can start to sound dubbed-on, and not at all natural.'

Again, the bird songs are incidental, extras in walk-on parts, painstakingly backgrounded and secondary to the main action – and yet they are indispensable. Birdsong is context; without it, we find it that bit more difficult to make sense of the world.

Earlier in this chapter, I casually dropped in the word 'biophony'. It's a terrific word, and we should all get used to using it. It was coined in 1998 by the sound recordist Bernie Krause in his book *Into a Wild Sanctuary* to describe the totality of sounds created by living things (other than people) in a given habitat – so that might include bird-song, the stridulations of crickets, the humming of bees, the barking of foxes, and a whole lot of other noises. Krause later rounded out his acoustic glossary by adding the terms *geophony* (noises made by the earth and elements: the chortling of a stream, say, or the rumbling of thunder) and *anthropophony* (noises made by people).

I got in touch with Krause after reading his last book, *The Great Animal Orchestra*. I was fascinated by his work in natural acoustics, and by how the concept of biophony might allow us to integrate the sounds we hear with the earth we tread. If we want to talk about birdsong and landscape – and if we want it to mean anything – we have to talk about biophony.

'Natural soundscapes', Krause writes, 'are the voices of whole ecological systems.'

Chatting over email (and across half a dozen time zones), I asked Krause how – over an evolutionary timescale – a bird might develop its songs and calls in response to the animals, birds and landscape around it; how a species might find its place in the biophony. 'It all depends on a combination of factors, such as topography, vegetation, the micro-climate, the time of day or night, season, humidity, altitude, temperature, atmospheric pressure, the geophony, and vocal organism mix,' he replied. Okay. This was likely to get complicated.

Krause explained to me the Acoustic Niche Hypothesis (ANH): the idea that each noise-making animal will evolve into a niche from where it can transmit the sounds it needs to transmit in order to survive. It will find a way to make its voice heard.

'If its voice is germane to its success, then it will need to find unimpeded channels to convey those signals,' Krause elaborated. 'Over time, and if there isn't some kind of natural disturbance, the definition of these niches tends to become more and more clear.'

There might be countless bioacoustic factors feeding into the noises a bird makes. An example Krause gives in his book is the way in which some species will wait until the surrounding landscape has been dried out by the sun before beginning to sing – warm, arid air will allow their voices to carry further. Others might make use of the resonant stillness of a lake for the same purpose. Birds like this really are playing the landscape like an instrument.

Frequency is important, too. For example, songs in which lower notes and whistles predominate are less liable to be broken up – 'degraded' – by vegetation than higher-pitched songs; however, low-frequency song suffers greater degradation when it's sung less than a metre or so from the ground.

It's all pretty complex stuff, but if the Acoustic Niche Hypothesis is correct then the birds will 'know' these things – that is to say, they'll have evolved to mostly sing low notes and whistles in thick vegetation, and to hit the higher notes in habitats where the cover is less dense.

And indeed, it seems that they *do* know these things, and much else besides: ambient noise, reverberation and interference all appear to have been factored in by natural selection during the evolution of many bird songs. South American antbirds, song sparrows in the US, little greenbuls in the central African rainforest and great tits in English woodland all show the variations we'd expect. The acoustic landscape has made its mark.

Talking to Krause, it seemed notable that those two emblematic songsters of ours, the skylark and the nightingale, both have songs that are heavy on geographical context: the skylark's is delivered from the summit of a towering display-flight, while the nightingale's always – in England, anyway – comes from dense undergrowth. I wondered how these contrasting factors might have affected the songs themselves. But Krause couldn't say.

'Context is everything', he agreed – but a biophony is a web, a tapestry of a thousand crisscrossing threads that is practically impossible to unpick. All we can say for sure is that, if a bird evolved in a British landscape, we really can hear a little bit of Britain in its song.

4

An Elusive Song

'Those who say birdsong is not music
are fools of the first water.'

– Anonymous naturalist,
quoted in Charles Hartshorne's *Born to Sing* (1973)

When the pheasant came crashing through the bus windscreen I might have taken it as a sign that I was on the right track. I was on my way to find out something the birds didn't want me to know.

The bus from Leeds to the British Library's northern outpost near the village of Boston Spa takes a winding A-road northwards through woodland and arable fields. It's a rustic, autumny landscape of rook and woodpigeon, beech and hawthorn; more browns in it than greens.

We were trucking along a straight stretch of road at perhaps 40mph when he rocketed from the hedgerow on our right, and met the glass of the windscreen with a *crack* rather than a *whump*; the impact – feet or bill or both, I suppose – was enough to smash a crazy web of fractures in the glass, give the driver the fright of his life ('*That's* never happened before', he said dully afterwards, through a cloud of cigarette smoke), and put the bus out of commission.

A half-hour wait at the roadside brought a replacement bus; I got off at Boston Spa – historic, well kept and eye-wateringly prosperous – and walked the rest of the way. Noisy detachments of jackdaws and starlings watchfully attended my progress.

I was going to the library because they had a copy of Walter Garstang's 1935 book *Songs of the Birds*. I hoped it might unlock birdsong for me. I hoped it might help me hear the music I'd been missing.

Garstang was an interesting man. He earned a small amount of fame as a scholar of marine invertebrates, a subject on which he also wrote humorous poetry (sample lines, from 'Oikopleura, Jelly Builder': 'A filter in front collects all the fine particles, / Micro-flagellates and similar articles').* If you think the name sounds familiar, it might be because we had a brush with Mr Garstang back

---

* After Garstang's death, these poems were published in a collection with the enchanting title *Larval Forms and Other Zoological Verses*.

in Chapter 2: Leeds University's Garstang building, where Peter Tickle and I subjected a partridge to indignities, is named after Walter.

He also cultivated a fine ear for birdsong. Songs, however, differ from marine invertebrates in that they cannot be netted, gutted and pickled in jars; music – if birdsong is music – is even more slippery. This, I think, bothered Garstang. His instinct was to share the music of the birds – the 'antiphonies, rondos and fantasias' of the thrushes, the 'canzonets and lyrics' of the finches and warblers – but to do that he had first to translate it into human terms.

We've been trying to do this with birdsong, one way or another, for centuries.

Every culture has its origin stories, its creation myths; music is no different, and many of these myths feature birds. A Lakota Sioux legend tells of how a young hunter was shown by a bird how to make the first flute. In ancient Rome, the philosopher-poet Lucretius wrote of how the first men learned music from the birds ('Thro' all the woods they heard the charming noise / Of chirping birds, and try'd to frame their voice / And imitate. Thus birds instructed man'). In Christian Europe, it was sometimes argued that Eve was driven to create music through jealousy of the birds' songs; St Gregory, meanwhile, was said to have been taught the form of plainsong known as 'Gregorian chant' by a white dove.*

Traditions of this sort help to explain why we treasure the songs of birds like the robin and nightingale (rather than, say, the magpie and the herring gull). We like bird songs that have clear tones, repeated phrases, and clearly distinct notes; we like bird songs that remind us of our own music.

For various reasons – some physiological (to do with the limits of our hearing), others cultural – most human music is based on variations of five to twelve notes. These constitute only a tiny fraction of the billions of *potential* notes that lie between, for instance, a low C and a high C, but they're the ones we use. Generally, we play or sing the notes as discrete sounds, within a structured scale. When we think something 'sounds like music', that's usually what we're hearing.

Birds, by this standard, don't sing music. A 2012 study in the journal *Animal Behaviour* found that only

* It may be that the first musical instruments were made in an attempt to toot and whistle as the birds do, and indeed the oldest known instrument – a 40,000-year-old flute, discovered in Germany in 2008 – was whittled from the bone of a bird. It's probably best not to read too much into this, though: the bird in question was a vulture, which isn't known for its song.

occasionally does birdsong play by human rules. Robert Zatorre of McGill University in Montreal analysed the song of the nightingale wren – eighty-one nightingale wrens, in fact – to see whether the bird's notes followed the same pattern as the diatonic, pentatonic and chromatic scales familiar to human musicians (for comparison, he also subjected J. S. Bach's *Six Suites for Unaccompanied Cello* to the same analysis). Out of 243 songs, Zatorre found that only six used similar 'harmonic intervals' – that is, the differences in pitch between different notes – as *our* music. This suggests that hearing music in birdsong is simply a projection of our inbuilt biases – like seeing faces in the shapes of clouds.

Perhaps there was a time when birdsong and human music had a closer relationship than they do today, just as there was a time when the common ancestor of both birds and humans walked the earth; we've just drifted apart. Perhaps we never really got over the split. It seems that ever since then we've been trying to find ways to close the gap – to make birdsong ours again.

Of course, in many ways the whole *point* of birdsong is that it's beyond our grasp. It's fleeting, evanescent; you might as well try to take a fistful of morning mist. But that hasn't stopped us trying. One way of doing that, we thought, was to imitate it. If we could make their music a part of our music, we could, in a sense, take ownership of it. Perhaps the lines of a composer's stave could do for birdsong what the bars of a birdcage do for a bird (we'll talk more about actual birdcages in the next chapter).

❦

Any respectable medieval musicologist, fished from the grave to address one of the most vexed questions in birdsong study, would tell you definitively that birdsong is not music. In the Middle Ages, this wasn't a question of personal opinion; it practically amounted to a logical syllogism. Music is a product of the rational mind; birds do not have rational minds; therefore, birds cannot make music.

This idea was applied to human singers, too. The human voice, after all, was a pipe on which pretty much anyone could play a tune; far better – far more sophisticated, and therefore far more *human* – to master the sackbut, or the gittern, or the harpsichord.

In her book *Sung Birds*, Professor Elizabeth Eva Leach makes the point that, to the musicologists of the Middle Ages, comparisons between human singers and songbirds as masters of 'virtuoso, spontaneous, naturally talented vocal production' weren't invalid, exactly – they just had an unfortunate whiff of degradation about them.

Song of this kind was, by implication, subhuman, 'and therefore perhaps morally suspect'. 'The singer's skill was being denigrated,' she explained to me. 'The singer has been turned into a sort of unthinking machine – or an unthinking bird.'

The response of the singers was to double down: they began to deliberately incorporate the impulsive, untutored rhythms of birdsong into the songs they sang. It was a plain message to snotty composers: *transcribe* that, *if you can*.

But the idea had taken hold. Wild music could be beautiful, but human music was simply, by definition, better. Birdsong and human music share the same seven notes, the eighteenth-century musician Christian Friedrich Daniel Schubart admitted – 'but what man has done with them!'

Walter Garstang describes the blackbird as 'the Beethoven of the birds': an irresistible virtuoso. It's unlikely that the compliment would mean much to the average blackbird, but Beethoven himself might have appreciated it. His 1808 Symphony No. 6 in F major, commonly known as the 'Pastoral', incorporates the calls of the quail, the cuckoo and the nightingale in its musical representation of a day in the countryside – except, of course, that it really does no such thing, but instead uses a flute, an oboe and two clarinets to create approximations of these noises. It's human music, Beethoven's music; it's wonderful, like a mechanical nightingale is wonderful, but it isn't birdsong.

Even more obliquely avian is the final movement of Beethoven's Symphony No. 2 in D major. Some listeners say that they can hear the rhythm of a Cetti's warbler's song in the movement's animated opening notes; who knows, it may even be that Beethoven intended them to. (The writer David Turner has speculated that the phantom warbler in this symphony lies 'somewhere in the twilight zone between chance and conscious imitation'; an ornithologist's reading, made with a well-thumbed breeding-bird atlas to hand, might be that the Cetti's warbler, *Cettia cetti*, wasn't known to breed in Beethoven's German homeland until the 1970s, so it seems unlikely that the young maestro heard one singing its ear-splitting song in between recitals in Bonn or Vienna.) Again, though, this isn't birdsong – and the point is, it's not *meant* to be birdsong. It's meant to be music.

There's a famous story by Hans Christian Andersen called 'The Nightingale'. It tells of a Chinese emperor who invites a nightingale to perform at his court. The obliging bird sings 'so sweetly that the tears came into the emperor's eyes'; she becomes a celebrity, and is kept in a cage in the emperor's household. Then a gift arrives for the emperor: 'an artificial nightingale made to look like a living one, and covered all over with diamonds, rubies, and sapphires'. The clockwork nightingale – which will sing only waltzes, over and over – wins the favour of the fickle emperor, and the real nightingale, neglected, returns to her home in the greenwood.

The fable, written in 1833, has a Romantic moral: we are supposed to see that the emperor is a fool, and that a wind-up toy is no match for a flesh-and-feather nightingale. But to the seventeenth-century mind, the emperor has exactly the right idea. The clockwork nightingale is a thing of rationality, of human ingenuity and scientific principles; of *course* it is better than a mere bird. By the same reasoning, composers of the pre-Romantic age concluded that musical instruments represented the height of human artistic skill. So when a birdsong craze gripped the cultured classes of Western Europe in the eighteenth century, it makes sense that the songs so highly prized were produced not by the avian syrinx but by springs, pins and cogs.

The period saw the production of a host of exquisite musical gewgaws that might have been collectively marketed under the slogan 'Nature, Only Better'. Clocks, snuffboxes, bracelets and walking sticks were all made to emit tinkling variations on the 'birdsong' theme.

The Swiss Jacob Frisard created a 'gold, enamel and split-seed pearl *oiseau chantant* and musical portrait box', complete with a 'bird with close detail banded and layered feathered plumage in hues of electric blue, deep black, lime green, turquoise and white-tip highlights, the iridescent highlights in subtle orange and dark green to wings and front, when actuated, moving body, head, ivory beak, wings and tailfeather to continuous birdsong'.* (The description comes from the website of the auctioneer who sold this trinket for £181,250 in 2012.)

This is kind of what humans always do: we see something we like, we make a grab for it, and then more often than not things get completely out of hand. We don't know when to stop. It's positive, in a lot of ways; I, in any case, *like* complexity, ingenuity, richness and invention. It's just that, in making use of things in this way, we have a tendency to lose sight of where they came from in the first place – and of what it was we liked about them. We labour so long in our workshops (tweezering split-seed pearls on to our *oiseaux chantants*) that we never step out of the door to hear a real bird's song. Just as we apply the final full-stop to our pastoral ode, the last British skylark

---

* The song actually played was a refrain entitled 'The Shepherd and the Clouds', not – as far as we know – a melody native to the repertoire of any wild bird.

goes extinct. We get carried away. Sometimes it's best to just leave the birds to it.

Birds, though, won't stick to scales, won't sing on cue, can't read music, and are liable to crap all over the concert hall. What's more, as we've seen, birdsong is tied in tightly with a lot of other things – ideas of place, of nature, of biophony – and is diminished when it's made to stand alone. Birdsong, in short, comes with baggage.

But maybe we could work with that.

The wooded ridge known as Gianicolo or 'Janiculum' is one of Rome's highest eminences. West of the Tiber, south of the Vatican, it commands an unsurpassed view of the Eternal City and the hills beyond; the paired domes of Santa Maria di Loreto and Santissimo Nome di Maria, the knock-your-eye-out white marble bulk of the Monumento a Vittorio Emanuele II, the lesser summits of the Chiesa di Santa Maria in Campitelli (tiled, earthy, russet) and the Tempio Maggiore di Roma (aluminium, squared-off, unwashed green-to-grey). It might be a good spot to watch the autumn murmurations of Rome's starlings, which furl and unfurl over the ancient rooftops at dusk and make the streets slick with their faeces; you might pick out the pale m-shapes of the city's notoriously fierce yellow-legged gulls in prowling flight. In summer, you might, here among the beech trees, stone pines and cypresses, hear the song of a nightingale – and, if you do, you might think of Ottorino Respighi.

Respighi's orchestral 'tone poem' *Pini di Roma* – 'Pines of Rome' – premiered in the city in 1924. The third movement of the piece is called 'Pines of the Janiculum'; about six minutes in, as the strings subside, a strange noise bubbles out over the high hum of a solo clarinet. It's a nightingale, a real one, or, at least, a recording of a real one.* This is thought to be the first notable classical work to incorporate, rather than imitate, a bird's song. It feels like a shift in the balance; an acknowledgement that perhaps birdsong – *real* birdsong, unimproved by a composer's ingenuity – had a place in music after all.

Supposedly, Respighi roped in the real-life nightingale after his attempts to replicate the bird's song with the 'high woodwind' instruments (clarinet, oboe, piccolo and flute) ended in failure – a convincing nightingale impersonation proved just too difficult to pull off. It's a crowd-pleasing moment in a sentimental piece of music

---

* The music writer Richard Dyer speculates that the 1924 premiere used the recording made by Karl Reich, whose 78rpm disc 'Record Made by a Captive Nightingale' was released in 1910.

(Respighi's notes describe the imagined scene: 'There is a thrill in the air: the pine-trees of the Janiculum stand distinctly outlined in the clear light of the full moon.') Many critics see Respighi's nightingale as a rather crude stunt; some even argue that the heavy-handed imagery and lack of subtlety in the work align Respighi with the values of Italian fascism (it's certainly true that Mussolini was a big fan).

Personally – and somewhat to my surprise – I quite like it. It feels to me that the orchestra makes plenty of room for the nightingale's *tweet-tweet-tweet, jug-jug-jug, teerew-teerew-tee rew* and so on; I expected the effect to be jarring, like hearing a tune in one key whistled over an instrumental line being played in another, but Respighi – unable to take hold of the bird's song, as Beethoven did, and bend it to his will – instead makes the orchestra do the work of accommodating, complementing and responding to the bird. It feels like the nightingale is in charge.

The singers of the fourteenth century would surely have approved of this inversion of the hierarchy. But the debate there, in the fraught rehearsal-rooms of medieval Europe, was about melody, about the notes the singers sang. Something more subtle is going on here – and has been going on since Beethoven. Let's listen again to that

Beethoven piece, the 'Pastoral' Symphony. Why are the birds there – the quail, the cuckoo, the nightingale? It's only partly about their melodies (or rather, the melodies they inspired Beethoven to create). This isn't only an exercise in the clever manipulation of notes and intervals; it's about a mood, and a sense of place – birdsong was the junction at which these things, along with music, intersected.

Beethoven – though a master of classical technique – infused his music with *Gefühl*, emotion; he described the 'Pastoral' as 'an expression of feeling' (Wordsworth and Coleridge, riding the same thundering wave of artistic Romanticism, were doing much the same thing in poetry).

After Beethoven, musicians felt able to move still further away from classical convention. So birdsong doesn't conform to classical ideas of what music should sound like? So a nightingale doesn't stick to a C-major scale, so a blackcap doesn't seem to grasp the idea of a 4/4 time signature? Who cares?

It took a while, of course. Old ideas are stubborn and hard to shift. But it's intriguing to wonder how much earlier Respighi's nightingale might have made an appearance had the Romantics had access to an Edison cylinder machine.

The poet and wildlife writer Matt Merritt has described the song thrush as a 'jazz improviser' (as distinct from the classically inclined blackbird). It's surprising, really, that birdsong – so often a recklessly free-form jam – hasn't featured more heavily in the jazz canon (the provocative question 'is this music?' might just as readily be asked of jazz as of birdsong, after all).

But in 2004 the Bristol-born saxophonist Evan Parker – a leading light in avant-garde jazz since the 1960s – collaborated with soundscapists John Coxon and Ashley Wales to fuse his sax improvisations with the untutored music of songbirds (and the squawking brass of urban seagulls) on the record *Evan Parker With Birds*. I don't pretend to know much about jazz; I struggle, I suppose, without stability, structure and sense (this might be why I've often found it difficult to hear the music in birdsong). But the concept of the soundscape seems important here.

Here, again, we see the tethering of birds to place, birdsong as an integral part of a local biophony. The place in question might be the 'hyperreal jungle' of Parker's record, or it might be a real place, a real habitat – a place 'Between the Saltmarsh and the Sea', say. That's the opening song from the album *Bonxie* by the indie-folk band Stornoway. The album incorporates twenty recordings of bird songs, calls and, in the case of one track, the curious jabbering noise made by the tail feathers of the snipe during its 'drumming' flight display.*

'The natural world and the outdoors generally have always been a big part of our music,' Brian Briggs, the band's vocalist, tells me. 'With the musical arrangements in the songs we've tried our best to build on the lyrical settings and the general mood and atmosphere. On previous records we've tried to do that with instruments, and on this one we thought we'd go one step further, because we had songs set out on the saltmarsh where I live, here in Gower, and songs set in the uplands. We tried to immerse our listener even more in that setting by bringing some of the real atmosphere you might hear in those places.'

I called Briggs because I wanted to know how a singer feels about birdsong, and I knew that Stornoway was one of a few modern bands whose members were birdwatchers as well as pop stars (others include Elbow and Guillemots†). In fact I was only partly right: 'It's just

---

* The list in full: Brent goose, chiffchaff, oystercatcher, curlew, greenshank, redshank, herring gull, skylark, red grouse, snipe, blackbird, great tit, short-toed treecreeper, starling, wren and – hurrah! – blackcap.

† Guillemots, bless them, provided one of the few moments in modern history when a birdwatcher was allowed to feel more hip and on-trend than a *Guardian* music reviewer. Opening his review of

me,' Briggs smiles when I ask if his bandmates share his passion for birds. Briggs has an Oxford degree in biological sciences and a PhD in ornithology; he volunteers as a warden at the Wildfowl and Wetlands Trust reserve in Llanelli. I hoped he'd have a lot of wise observations to make about the common ground between avian music and our music – but in fact he doesn't.

'People have asked me about the influence of birdsong on my music, and it doesn't really have an influence; it's not a direct thing,' he says. 'You can appreciate the noise of a bird singing, but it's so distant from the creation of pop music. The fact that there's only a couple of birds that people have well-known phrases for – like the yellowhammer's *little-bit-of-bread-and-no-cheese* – shows that there's very few birds that have musical songs that fit into what we hear as music.'

For Briggs, learning birdsong wasn't, as I'd imagined, something along the lines of a young Mozart hearing a concerto played once and then sitting down to give a note-perfect recital. It was, rather, a slog. 'I found it difficult', he cheerfully admits.

---

the band's debut album, Dave Simpson asked, 'Is that pronounced "gillmots" or "gee-mo"?' As any binocular-toting bird nerd knows, it is in fact 'gill-ee-motts', with a hard 'g'.

Wytham Woods, a pocket of mixed forest west of Oxford that has been used in bird study since the 1950s, was a rich training-ground.

'I was inspired by my trainer and by the people around me who could identify the birds by their songs. I decided I wanted to be able to do that. It opened up this extra world. In the woods, you hear birds more than you see them, and so it made me feel a lot more immersed in that habitat and able to feel more involved in what was around.'

For Briggs and Stornoway, the noises of birds are bricks in a process of world-building. It's not about *their* music and *our* music; it's about soundscapes, and again, that sense of place. In this context, when we ask 'what does the bird's song mean?' we don't give an answer like 'freedom' or 'exultation' or 'challenge'; we might say 'Wytham Woods in the spring', or 'a saltmarsh in winter', or 'a seabird colony in the breeding season'. It's about what it means to *us*.

'I love the way bird calls announce that you have arrived at another place,' the composer Dominic Crawford Collins has written. 'The song of certain birds in a particular location provides a kind of fifth dimension to your experience of a place.'

Real birds – in the form of recorded birdsong – have found their way into many other kinds of music since Respighi's day. The Finnish composer Einojuhani Rautavaara worked calls including those of the whooper swan and shorelark into his wintry 1972 *Cantus Arcticus*; the advance of technology allowed Rautavaara to tinker with the shorelark's song (usually a bright, seesawing twitter), pulling it down two octaves to create what he called a 'ghost bird'. The work is divided into movements entitled 'The Marsh', 'Melancholy' and 'Swans Migrating' – again, this is about feeling, landscape and atmosphere; it's a soundtrack to the composer's sense of place.

Per Nørgård's 1985 *D'Monstrantz vöögeli*, meanwhile, pits human singers against recorded birds; as the piece progresses, the bird recordings are slowed down, and brought within reach of the human voice – at the end, the singers perform surreal poetry to the song of the spotted nightingale thrush. Birdsong here seems to be doing something new: it's present in the music not just as something to listen to but something to think about.

In effect, it's conceptual art – the singing bird here is an unmade bed in the Tate, a urinal in the MOMA. As Beatrice Wood said of the urinal Marcel Duchamp submitted for exhibition in 1917, Nørgård 'creates a new thought for the object'. Context, once again, is the key; really, we're still talking about place. Where am I hearing this sound? Why here, why now?

There is more tinkering – more improving on nature, and more conceptualism – in Jonathan Harvey's complex and acclaimed *Bird Concerto with Pianosong* (2001). Harvey's goal was to achieve 'contact between worlds': 'If the songs and objects of the score can bring some inkling of how it might feel to be a human in the mind of a bird, or vice-versa, then I would be happy,' he wrote. It sounds like an impossible dream – but even if it *is* impossible, that never deterred Coleridge, or George Meredith, or Christina Rossetti, or any of the poets who pursued that same dream: of feeling, somehow, what a singing songbird feels.

The electroacoustic *Concerto* requires the pianist to play not only the piano but, via a synthesiser keyboard, a suite of digitised bird songs, creating a 'conversation' between the two forms – the two worlds – of music. In the best-known version of the work, the deft piano trills of the Japanese virtuoso Hideki Nagano (accompanied by a seventeen-strong instrumental ensemble) are jostled by the songs of the indigo bunting, the orchard oriole, the golden-crowned sparrow and some forty other Californian songbirds. I like the sense of compromise here; the idea of a creative mind-meld between pianist and songbird.

Ultimately, though, we *can't* listen like a sparrow or an oriole listens. The US scientist Alison Greggor wrote a paper entitled 'Why Can't We Love Like an Albatross?';* she concluded that it's because we aren't albatrosses – because 'our experience of love is just as much part of being human as having two legs'. I think the same applies to our experience of birdsong (there's just no escaping the limits of our humanness, however much they might chafe sometimes). But there's great value in any attempt to open diplomatic channels, so to speak, between the 'two worlds' Harvey talks about.

Harvey's *Concerto* was intended as a homage to the French composer Olivier Messiaen, who died in 1992. Messiaen never, as far as I can see, used 'real' bird noises in his compositions, and yet he's remembered as modern music's greatest interpreter of birdsong. He did, in a sense, use recordings: fascinated by birdsong, he attempted what had once been considered impossible, and created transcriptions – that is, musical notations – of the songs and calls he heard. His works, as a consequence, are rippled with bird impersonations: the famous *Le Réveil des oiseaux* ('The Awakening of the Birds') imitates a dawn chorus

---

* My wife and I love Greggor's paper so much we had it as one of the readings at our wedding – making it *quite* clear from the outset that neither of us would be prepared to make annual thousand-mile ocean voyages before reuniting on clifftops to perform beak-clacking mating dances.

of blackcap, nightingale, song thrush, chaffinch, great spotted woodpecker and many more; one movement of his *Chronochromie* features eighteen violins, each playing a different 'bird song'. There are sites online that allow you to listen to real bird recordings alongside Messiaen's musical remakes: from the gong and woodwind of the prairie chicken to the chiming piano of the cardinal, you have to admit it's a neat trick.

For Messiaen, as with Harvey, birdsong was a means of connection – a ladder into the treetops, or higher still: into the spiritual plane, into something we (if we were that way inclined) might call heaven. This is birdsong as a stepping stone to higher things, a key to the doors of perception.

So is this their music, or our music? It's sort of a translation, I suppose: not a literal, Google-translate translation, but something more like a literary translation – an interpretation not of what's said but what's *meant*. The problem is, of course, that neither Jonathan Harvey nor Olivier Messiaen nor anybody else knows what the indigo bunting means; what the orchard oriole is getting at when he says *ch-ch*, or *hey you*, or *twee-ohh!* Perhaps not even the orchard oriole knows. Perhaps the question itself doesn't mean much. We can still say only what birdsong means *to us*.

Perhaps birdsong is best listened to on its own terms.

In the spring of 1881, Richard Jefferies – nature writer, novelist and jobbing journo – stood in the countryside south-west of London and listened to the birds. Some you can still hear there: sparrows, say ('the chirp has a tang in it, a sound within a sound, just as a piece of metal rings'), or chaffinches ('the chaffinch now has a note very much like one used by the yellow-hammer'). Others – turtle dove, great grey shrike, wryneck ('the wryneck's *kie-kie-kie* reminds one of the peacock's strange scream') – are in much shorter supply than they were.*

Jefferies also heard nightingales, there in the leafy green country between Esher and Surbiton, Chessington and Thames Ditton. One, he wrote, often duetted with a sedge warbler: 'The one often sings in the branches above, while the other chatters in the underwood beneath.'

---

* Though one will still hear 'strange screams' there, and these, like the peacock's, will have an Indian inflection: the oh-so-English Surrey suburbs are now a stronghold of the wild rose-ringed parakeet, a vivid green parrot that since the 1970s has been adding its voice – a loud chittering, or a shrill *kii-ah!* – to our songbird chorus.

Jefferies goes on to describe walking through the fields bordering a farmhouse called The Waffrons. Some forty-odd years after Jefferies took his spring stroll there, The Waffrons – no longer attached to a working farm – was rented by the Harrison family. The Harrison sisters, Beatrice and May, were celebrated cellists. In the early 1920s, they were visited by the Bradford-born composer Frederick Delius; it was at The Waffrons that he began work on his Cello Concerto. Beatrice recalled him writing music in the garden of the house: 'He was literally bathed in golden sunlight among the flowers . . . The crystal air was vibrating with the chant of many birds, the skylark floating upwards to the clouds in an unseen world, the white doves beating their wings through the air, the blackbird, the robin, the thrush, the tiny tits, even the little jenny-wren, all seemed to vie with each other to charm him.'

Reading, now, that parts of Delius's concerto are literally impossible to play – 'the top notes cannot be maintained while playing the semiquavers,' Julian Lloyd Webber complained – it's hard not to wonder whether the composer was influenced by the birdsong around him: it's madly high pitch, its hemidemisemiquavers.

Delius certainly loved birdsong. He 'almost lived' in his garden at Grez, in France; Beatrice wrote: 'I am sure that he heard glorious music from the invisible air as it wafted around him.' She herself was a keen bird-keeper, and later presented Delius with two cage birds: a Harz Roller canary (which he named 'Tommy', after the conductor Sir Thomas Beecham) and a Chinese nightingale. The Chinese nightingale is properly known as the red-billed leiothrix, and isn't related to our own *Luscinia* at all – but it was with the nightingales of England that Beatrice Harrison would soon become indelibly associated.

It happened, at first, quite by accident, not long after the Harrisons had left The Waffrons for a house near Oxted in east Surrey known as Foyle Riding. The house had splendid grounds, maintained by a gardener Beatrice remembered for his foul language, gentle blue eyes and 'the bandiest legs I have ever seen'. In the spring, Beatrice took her cello into the bluebell woods. 'I began to play, very lazily, all the melodies I loved best, and to improvise on them,' she recalled.

During Rimsky-Korsakov's 'Chanson indoue', some-one else joined in: 'Suddenly a glorious note echoed the notes of the cello . . . I then trilled up and down the instrument, up to the top and down again: the voice of the bird followed me in thirds! I had never heard such a bird's song before – to me it seemed a miracle. I just played on and on.' It was, the potty-mouthed gardener confirmed, a nightingale – returned to Foyle Riding, he said, 'after so long'.

After that first duet, Beatrice took to playing in the woods every night, 'listening to the heavenly bird, my only audience being the rabbits, and once a tiny shrew came and sat on my foot'. Come June, the nightingale took off for its African wintering grounds, and the gardens fell silent – 'but the cello never forgot the voice of the nightingale'.

The following spring, Beatrice decided that her private audiences with the nightingale weren't enough; this was music she wanted the world to hear. She put a call through to Sir John Reith at the BBC (a fairly new enterprise at the time). Would the Corporation be willing to stage a live broadcast from Foyle Riding? Reith was very dubious at first – but 'I knew,' Beatrice wrote, 'that the good God wished the world to hear the duet of the cello and the nightingale.' After a 'hard tussle', the BBC gave in; a reluctant recording crew was despatched to the bluebell woods.

The Beeb's scepticism was understandable: setting up an outside broadcast of this kind would be awkward and technically challenging – no one had yet broadcast the music of a wild bird. Besides, how could they be sure that the nightingale would turn up and sing as scheduled?

By around nine o'clock at night, Foyle Riding was wired for sound. Beatrice crept into the woods with her cello, and set herself up on the edge of a ditch ('half in and half out of it, quite crooked'). Then she began to play.

'I played for what seemed like hours, praying all the time,' she wrote in her memoir, *The Cello and the Nightingales*. 'I knew that the exquisite voice was there, under a thicket of oak leaves, ready to sing to his little wife.'

You can imagine the impatience of the sound crew. The shyness of the nightingale was only one of their problems. The wires strung through the woods were being nibbled by rabbits; a neighbour's donkey seemed to be hell-bent on sabotage, first braying noisily and then buffeting an engineer into a ditch.

Then it happened: 'At about quarter to eleven on the night of the 19th of May, 1924, the nightingale burst into song.' In living rooms across the country, nightingale song, framed by the cello's hum, came crackling out of wireless receiving-sets. Again, Rimsky-Korsakov's 'Chanson indoue' seemed to be the bird's favourite: 'He blended with it so perfectly. I shall never forget his voice that night.'

The broadcast, the BBC reported, was heard by around a million people. Beatrice was told that people who didn't have wirelesses – plenty didn't, in 1924 – listened to the duet on friends' sets, over the telephone, and that the music of the Savoy Opera fell silent as the nightingale's song broke from the loudspeakers.

Beatrice and the BBC (and the nightingale, of course) repeated the performance the following week – and then the following spring. HMV pressed a record of the duet. The public, meanwhile, 'went completely mad': Beatrice received sacks of fan mail – often addressed to 'the Lady of the Nightingales, England' – and visitors began to arrive at Foyle Riding quite literally by the busload. The hospitable Harrisons chartered coaches from the East End and Stepney so that 'hundreds of little children' – many of whom had never seen a bluebell, never mind heard a nightingale – could enjoy late-night tea parties; Henry Ford stopped by, and, according to Beatrice, was baffled when the Harrisons refused his offer to buy Foyle Riding, bluebells, nightingales and all. Beatrice recalled being stopped in the street by well-wishers asking: 'Have you got the nightingale with you, Miss?'

It's quite a coincidence that Respighi's nightingale took its first bow in Rome in the year of the first BBC broadcast from Foyle Riding. It's an intriguing comparison, too: the recorded song of the nightingale cranked into gear amid the violins and stiff shirt-fronts of the

Teatro Augusteo, against the 'live' version – Beatrice's nightingale, singing what it wants, when it wants, in a Surrey woodland.

As you'd expect, Beatrice's nightingale is less compliant than Respighi's. His backing music, after all, wasn't designed to accommodate a nightingale's song (although Rimsky-Korsakov did try to transcribe birdsong, and included melodies inspired by his pet bullfinch in his operas *The Snow Maiden* and *Mlada*). The nightingale on the HMV recording – you can, of course, find it on YouTube – does seem to follow, in a rough sort of way, the pitch of Beatrice's cello, but the point is that he doesn't *have* to. His song hasn't been edited or AutoTuned to meet a composer's needs; the nightingale, daft as it sounds, has creative autonomy here. Just as Beatrice is improvising on Rimsky-Korsakov's themes, the nightingale is riffing on the tunes he learned as a fledgling.

It's a true duet, which means that, unlike 'Pines of the Janiculum', it's a two-way street: this nightingale – a musician, where Respighi's was an instrument – can hear Beatrice's music, just as she can hear the nightingale. So we get to flip around the question we've been asking – 'What do we hear when the birds sing?' – and ask instead, what did the nightingale hear in the song of the cello?

The cello obviously stimulated him – but did it infuriate him, make him angry, make him want to drive the intruding cello (Beatrice called it 'Peter') from his territory? Was he intrigued, did he want to imitate and learn the cello's song? Or did the music push his buttons in some fundamental nightingale way for which we have no analogue, no point of comparison?

We'll probably never know, of course. But we can hear in the recordings of Beatrice and the nightingale a coming-together of worlds quite unlike that envisaged by Jonathan Harvey in his *Bird Concerto with Pianosong*. Human music, the music of Rimsky-Korsakov, Beatrice Harrison and the cello, takes a modest step backwards, there in the Surrey bluebell wood; the nightingale's music, birdsong, *their* music, is for once allowed equal billing.

The British Library at Boston Spa is a sprawling complex of car parks, signboards, square-edged blocks of offices and storerooms. It reminds me of a hospital. As I followed the arrows to the reading room I thought of the poor pheasant we'd left behind us on the A-road (only one bird, of course, and the pheasant's *caark* isn't much of a song – but right now the countryside hasn't much music to spare).

Few birds were singing; it was November, bright and cold. There were rowans in bright berry beside the path, but no redwings or chittering waxwings feeding on them.

I found birdsong, instead, between the tatty green covers of Garstang's *Songs of the Birds*.

The greenfinch sings four bars of rapid-fire music in 2/4 time. A thrush and a blackbird duet in 3/8 time, like a fast waltz or a mazurka. The great tit sings *forte*, strong, loud, as in, say, the introduction to Tchaikovsky's *Swan Lake Suite*; the coal tit's note is *dolce*, sweet, like a Chopin prelude. It's all notated, neatly, in formal staves. There are 'lyrics' to the music, too (or a libretto, if you prefer) – twitter, twitter twitter, *chow, chow, chow*, and so on.

Walter Garstang was a scientist, but *Songs of the Birds* is really, I think, about music. He died in 1949, just as sonograms were beginning to transform the scientific study of birdsong – but I'm not sure Garstang's instincts would have led him down that route anyway. On hearing birdsong, his reflex was to reach for a different language: that of key signatures and scales and spatters of black-inked notes. What he wanted to do was crack the code, find the signal amid the noise; he wanted to translate birdsong into something we could all make sense of, so that we could all hear its music.

I don't think he quite pulled it off – but then, I'm not sure it can be done.

What we've been trying to do, all along, is separate the birdsong from the bird – to isolate it, like a scarce chemical, and fuse it into compounds and alloys of our own. But I'm just not sure it works like that. Birdsong on its own is elusive, evasive, evanescent; it always seems, somehow, to slip between our fingers.

A song I didn't recognise (remember that I'm not very good at this) was pealing in the twilit car park when I left the library's reading room. I picked out the singer, eventually, on the brim of a prefab outbuilding. It was a pied wagtail. Wagtails, in my experience, tend to arrive in a great hurry, making a sort of loud, piping *peep*, and then run about in all directions, looking busy. I hadn't heard one sing before, not like this, merrily, even giddily, and not in November. I remember that the wagtail, long-bodied, dainty, neat and perfect as a sharpened pencil, walked up and down the brim of the building as he sang, like a character in a musical. I don't remember his song.

5

A Captive Melody

I know why the caged bird sings, ah me,

When his wing is bruised and his bosom sore –

When he beats his bars and would be free . . .

– Paul Laurence Dunbar,

'Sympathy' (1899)

So what if we *don't* separate birdsong from the birds? What if we let the birds keep hold of it – but we, in turn, keep hold of the birds?

Bird-keeping can be traced back around five thousand years: the Sumerians of southern Mesopotamia, the first civilisation we know of to keep written records, had a word in their language for 'birdcage' ('subura'). In the fifth century BC, the Persian physician Ctesiphon wrote that certain captive birds could speak in human voices (and that birds reared in Persia could learn to speak fluent Greek); in 327 BC, when attempting to conquer India, two of Alexander the Great's generals whiled away their downtime by trying to capture and cage the local parakeets. But none of these examples, as far as we know, is really to do with song.

A cluster of islands in the east Atlantic helped to change all that. *Las Canarias* – Tenerife, Fuerteventura, Gran Canaria, Lanzarote, La Palma, La Gomera and El Hierro – were named after the giant dogs (Latin *canis*) that were said to live there;* that name in turn was passed on to *Serinus canarius*, the canary-bird. Fourteenth-century Portuguese sailors found them in great numbers on the islands: small finches, greenish-yellow, with a vibrant chir-ruping song (going by eye, you might mistake it for a siskin or greenfinch; going by ear, you might think it was a souped-up chaffinch).

They were exotic, lively and attractive. They soon became a must-have fashion accessory for the elites of southern Europe. Portuguese efforts to export only male birds from the Canary Islands – an attempt to restrict supply, and maintain monopoly – ultimately faltered. (Male and female canaries are tricky to tell apart – besides, demand was simply too great to resist: when, in 1622, word reached Tuscany that a cargo of females

---

* Some believe that the indigenous people of the islands engaged in dog-worship; then again, it may be that the earliest visitors to the island saw monk seals basking on the shores, and mistook them for monstrous hounds.

had escaped from a shipwrecked trading vessel on Elba, a flotilla was despatched specifically to secure the birds. They were sold in Livorno – where Shelley would later meet his skylark – for, it's said, their weight in gold.)

The canary was never only a pet of the middle-classes. The little bird's association with working men and women had begun with the sailors of the Iberian peninsula; it soon found itself prized by workers far to the north, its value measured not in gold coins accrued but in lives saved. In the early eighteenth century, miners, first in the copper-fields of the Austrian Alps and later in the silver-mines of Germany's Harz Mountains, pressed the canary into service as an early-warning system.

In the chokingly confined spaces of the ore seams, deposits of carbon monoxide posed a deadly threat. Canaries, because of their thrumming heart rate and super-efficient breathing system, are more vulnerable to the effects of the gas than humans are; carbon monoxide has no smell, colour or taste, but it will leave a canary out cold on the floor of its cage before the toiling miner starts to feel the effects.

Imagine being a canary transported from the sunshine of La Palma or Tenerife to the grim metal mines of central Europe. But then, imagine being a labourer in those mines, and hearing, amid the darkness, dust, sweat and toil, the jaunty whistle-twitter-trill of a canary-bird.

The song, of course, was incidental to the canary's duties, but it didn't go unnoticed. The harsh granite upland of Harz was not only mining country – it was also songbird country. Breeders and traders in and around Innsbruck kept up a bustling traffic in bullfinches, gold-finches and chaffinches. The canary-bird was soon added to their stock-lists. It would never thrive as a wild species in northern Europe (in fact, save for a twentieth-century introduction in Hawaii, it has never established itself out-side the Canaries, the Azores and Madeira) but as a cage bird, a captive songster, it was soon famous across the world.

In the nineteenth century, Walt Whitman, the white-bearded wild man of American poetry, declared in verse that the song of his caged canary – 'thy joy-ous warble, / Filling the air, the lonesome room, the long forenoon' – delighted his soul no less than all the hard-won wisdom of 'mighty books'. His enthusiasm was by no means untypical; caged songbirds – whether canaries, wild finches imported from Europe, or native species such as mockingbirds, cardinals and grosbeaks – were hugely popular in US households.

Two Manhattan traders, German-born brothers

named Charles and Henry Reiche, were the principal players in America's canary trade. In the 1840s, they were selling some 2,000 canaries a year out of their bird shop in the borough's downmarket Bowery district. In 1849, they went after the new-found wealth of Gold Rush California, shipping 3,000 canaries cross-country and pocketing as much as $50 a bird for their troubles.

Whitman, 'son of Manhattan', knew the Bowery well – its theatres, its public houses, its auction shops and 'heaps of goods'; he wrote of strolling by Chatham Square, 'enveloped on all sides with hubbub, haste, and countless thousands of people'. The scholar Jerry Dennis argues that Whitman probably called in at the Reiches' place on Chatham Street to acquire his canary. He would have been one of many: by 1871, the Reiches were importing 48,000 canaries a year.

The canary diaspora, fanning out from those salt-washed, sun-burnt east Atlantic islands, also made landfall in England. Here, too, they were miners' fail-safes (in use as recently as 1986); here, too, they were genteel household accessories ('fitting companions for our parlors,' as Charles Reiche put it, 'delighting us with their charming and sweet harmony'). The arrival of the canary here in the late 1500s was, in many ways, a great relief to middle-class bird-keepers. Up until then, the nightingale

– champion songster that it was – had been the most popular cage bird. Nightingales, though, were a nightmare to look after: they demanded soft food (worms, grubs and so on) and their droppings made an atrocious mess. The seed-eating canary was a much more agreeable house guest, and was soon made to feel at home in the English drawing-room.

For all that they were deprived of their liberty, these birds were perhaps the fortunate ones. Canary-keeping was not the only songbird subculture to have taken hold here. Working-class England had its own bird-keeping traditions; these were dug deeply into the culture of the grimy inner cities, and they meant misery for the birds who were trafficked into them.

'You makes 'em werry hot,' explains the man with the liming-twigs tucked behind his ear, 'and you holds 'em close, so that the eyes may kitch the 'eat well, and that brings the scale on 'em.'

The man is a bird-catcher, and he is explaining how one might use red-hot needles to blind a chaffinch. Even when we leave the singing to the birds, it seems, we find ways to spoil everything.

James Greenwood was a roving journalist of the late Victorian era, known in his byline as 'the amateur casual' and specialising in the street life of London; a chapter in his 1874 book *In Strange Company*, from which the above line of dialogue is taken, sheds light on what Greenwood called 'The Art and Mystery of Song-Bird Torture'.

The concept of competitive birdsong originated in mainland Europe in the late Middle Ages (among humans, that is; songbirds have been taking part in competitive birdsong for as long as they've been songbirds). Records of *vinkensport* – 'finch sport' – in Flemish Belgium date back to the 1590s: merchants competed to see which finches (chaffinches, primarily) could utter the most calls in a given time period. For a long time, only aristocrats were permitted to catch and keep finches; only after 1795, when the occupying French repealed the hunting laws, did *vinkensport* in Flanders become the pastime of the common man.

The 'flourish' at the end of the chaffinch's song – the delivery of the cricket ball, in our mnemonic – was what the *vinkeniers* wanted to hear. They rendered it *susk-e-wiet*, although again the chaffinch's capacity to sing in dialect was noted: the Flemish maintained that chaffinches from the French-speaking Wallonia region of Belgium uttered a warped and ineligible form of the note.

Indeed, they still do. The popularity of *vinkensport* peaked surprisingly recently – in the 1970s and 1980s, the Flemish association of finch-owners had some 20,000 members – and Flanders still maintains a small but dedicated number of *vinkeniers*. One of them,* interviewed by a reporter from the *New York Times* in 2007, worried that interest in the historic pastime was flagging: 'I love the thrill of finching, the camaraderie, the sense of history,' he said. 'The trouble is that bird-singing is no longer seen as sexy.'

The 'sense of history' might have something to do with that.

In nineteenth-century London, finch contests were a hugely popular pastime of the urban working classes, and the East End was their heartland. As with the *vinkeniers* of Flanders – who would have been called 'bird fanciers' in Limehouse or Bow – the chaffinch or 'greypate' was the passerine of choice ('the gay chaffinch is to them the first of the feathered race,' wrote the naturalist W. H. Hudson. 'In fact, it may be said that he is first and the others

---

* Filip Santens, whose champion chaffinch 'Orban' could knock out more than 500 *susk-e-wiets* in 15 minutes. Another champion chaffinch, 'Schauvlieghe', logged an improbable high score of 1,278 *susk-e-wiets*, but his career was dogged by rumours of testosterone abuse.

nowhere'; James Greenwood, however, eavesdropped on one fancier 'bragging of his "slamming" goldfinch', and another reciting the sixty-four distinct notes of the linnet 'of which the only sentence I could make out was "*tollic, tollic, tollic, chew-chew-tew-wit-joey*"'). Birds were pitted against each other in head-to-head sing-offs, with money riding on the outcome; one report from 1896 describes a contest at the Cock and Bottle in Shoreditch in which the 'Kingsland Roarer' out-sang 'Shoreditch Bobby' by 240 *chuck-wee-dos** to 212.

James Greenwood found his own 'night with the Fancy' less than compelling. According to his account in *In Strange Company*, Greenwood made his way to a charitable event at the Tinker's Arms in Spicer Street, Bethnal Green, at which, it was promised, 'Mr Cullum will show his celebrated battling finch'. He was disappointed. Descending to the pub's stifling 'parlour', he found seventy-odd bird fanciers crammed into a space built for perhaps twenty-five, puffing on pipes amid smothering heat and a 'terrible fog' of tobacco-smoke. All had their own finches with them, caged and covered over with handkerchiefs; none of the birds, Greenwood noted, was at any point encouraged

---

* None of your fancy Continental *susk-e-wiets* here, thank you very much.

to sing. 'Why on earth the gentlemen who met to smoke their pipes could not have left their finches at home was altogether a puzzle,' he remarked. He put the question to a gruff Cockney acquaintance, who attributed it to the bird fanciers' 'flashness'. On this night, at least, this was not about song, but about status. Birdsong, as we've seen, is often about status.

W. H. Hudson wondered whether there might be more to the bird fanciers' passion for chaffinches than one-upmanship and bar-room bragging rights – whether chaffinch song had a greater power to stir the emotions of a human listener ('even an East Ender') than other bird songs – to 'wake that ancient wild nature that sleeps in us'. He concluded, reluctantly, that there was not. Bird fanciers were in it for the sport, and that was all; a champion chaffinch was not a natural wonder but a commodity.

Again, people heard in birdsong what they wanted to hear – in this case, nothing but a gambling opportunity. It may be that Hudson was wrong, and that some of the East End's bird fanciers really did find beauty – music, even – in a linnet's crisp, pinched trill or a goldfinch's metallic twitter; that's no doubt why the practice of keeping songbirds caught on in the first place. But sports and games – be they football, cricket or an innocent bout of chaffinch one-upmanship – have a way of being winnowed down over time to a brutal fundamental: winning. Or, once gambling is involved, *winnings*.

The Victorian traffic in songbirds was, in certain parts of London, big business. A good singer might change hands for up to 50 shillings (at a time when a bricklayer might take home perhaps 7 shillings for a six-day working week). Charles Darwin recorded in 1871 that, 'although the price of an ordinary male chaffinch is only sixpence, Mr Weir saw one bird for which the bird-catcher asked three pounds' – not quite Reiche brothers money, sure, but not to be sniffed at. Darwin added the fascinating detail that 'the test of a really good singer [is] that it will continue to sing whilst the cage is swung round the owner's head'.

London's bird trade was cruelly inhumane. James Greenwood didn't mince his words: 'The way in which certain of these newly caught little creatures are treated by the heartless ruffians into whose hands they fall is terrible beyond belief.'

He described a visit to a trader on Sclater Street in Shoreditch; as well as birds, the trader, a Mr Slammer, dealt in rats, mice, pigeons, ferrets and chickens – not to mention spurs for fighting cocks and shears for cropping the ears of terriers. Greenwood found linnets, goldfinches, greenfinches, redpolls and chaffinches packed into what he called 'black holes': filthy, dark, shit-caked cages, each perhaps a foot by ten inches. Cock birds – that is, singers, who might turn a profit – received better treatment, but 'better' here is highly relative. Cocks, Greenwood observed, were 'lodged seldom more than six or eight in a cage that would conveniently lodge one'; grim, but generous compared with the *sixty* hen finches that he saw confined to a single cage. Can you imagine the smell of such a place? The noise of it?

Greenwood marvelled at the birds' resilience. 'Cat's-meat sellers* with impunity combine the bird-dealing business with their proper one, and perch their "store cages", containing songsters of every kind – including that ethereal creature, the skylark – on mounds of feculent horseflesh in their shop-windows,' he wrote.

The practice of blinding or 'scaling' the eyes of captive finches in the belief that it enhanced their singing prowess – 'makes 'em stiddier at their work', as 'Nosey' Warren, the cruel Bethnal Green bird-catcher encountered by James Greenwood, put it[†] – was a further stain

---

* Who dealt in meat *for* cats – generally horsemeat acquired from the knacker's yard – rather than the meat *of* cats.

[†] Similarly, a 1636 Flemish source asserts that 'if the finch is blind, then he sings the best'.

on the reputation of 'the fancy'. Thomas Hardy's grave 1916 poem 'The Blinded Bird' expressed the pity many felt for songbirds subjected to the practice:

> Who hath charity? This bird.
> Who suffereth long and is kind,
> Is not provoked, though blind
> And alive ensepulchred?
> Who hopeth, endureth all things?
> Who thinketh no evil, but sings?
> Who is divine? This bird.

Hardy marvelled at the songbird's capacity to suffer the most gruesome hardships and yet to carry on singing, without (he supposed) resentment or despair. It's a view with which many might sympathise, and that many might find inspiring – but it doesn't quite sit right with me. It reduces birdsong to a cheery whistle, a tossed-off all's-well-with-the-world too-ra-loo, and birdsong, to a bird, is so much more than that. Even a *chuck-wee-do* can be a lament, or a curse, or a ringing 'screw you' to 'Nosey' Warren and his red-hot needles. A bird's song can be as complex and as dark as any Hardy novel.

It's often thought that the practice of blinding birds was stamped out in Europe thanks largely to a protest march by soldiers blinded in action in the First World War. However, the scholars Pieter Verstraete and Ylva Söderfeldt have found no first-hand evidence of any such demonstration, either in England or in Flanders; rather, they emphasise the impact of a 1901 petition submitted to the Belgian National Assembly by the blind pupils of the Brussels Royal Institute for Deaf-mutes and the Blind. In it, the pupils called for the 'barbarous custom of blinding little birds' to be outlawed. 'More than anyone,' they wrote, 'we know the horrors of the deep and perpetual night in which children, even men, plunge these innocent and charming creatures.' Belgium nevertheless resisted the push to outlaw the blinding of songbirds until 1928.*

Back in the East End, Sclater Street remained central to the trade in songbirds into the twentieth century; George Sims, writing before the war, reported that on Sundays 'nothing but birdcages are to be seen from roofs to pavement in almost every house'.

Today, Sclater Street, E1 – barely more than a backstreet connecting Brick Lane in the east with Bethnal

---

* In England in 1933, meanwhile, Beatrice Harrison – the 'Lady of the Nightingales' – held a fundraising festival at Foyle Riding, collecting 1,000 signatures in favour of a Bill outlawing the blinding of caged birds.

Green Road in the west – has a more upmarket feel; while the south side of the road is a raffish reach of brickwork, graffiti, fly-posters and rusted window grilles, the north is 'acquired for development' territory: ad boards promise swish apartments, coming soon; green-meshed scaffolding swathes the old four-storey town houses.

It's not too long a walk – twenty-five minutes or so, if you trust Google Maps – from Sclater Street to Victoria Park, in the district of Bow. You might hear the odd chaffinch singing on the way, in the Museum Gardens at Bethnal Green, perhaps, or in the coppiced willows of Weaver's Fields (over the chugging traffic of the A1209) – but to an East End bird fancier, Victoria Park was the place to be. On a Sunday morning in springtime, Hudson recalled, 'many chaffinch fanciers may be met with; even on working days I have met as many as a dozen men slouching about among the shrubberies . . . in quest of a wild bird for his favourite to challenge and sing against'.

There was more to the life of a captive chaffinch than reeking pub parlours and fetid pet-shop cages – not much more, but more. If a singer was to retain his prize-winning vigour and tunefulness, he had to be exposed to wild chaffinch song; so it was that Hudson's acquaintances took to the shrubberies of Bow, birdcages in hand. Songbirds are students. They learn, as young-sters, from the birds around them (give or take a certain degree of genetic disposition to favour the songs of their own species). If you want your chaffinch to nail that note-perfect *chuck-wee-do*, you need to make sure he learns from the best – that is, wild chaffinches.

Birdsong, though, is a two-way street. The song of a wild chaffinch might be used to train a captive bird; the song of a captive bird could just as effectively be used to manipulate a wild chaffinch for a different, darker purpose.

Few songbirds can resist a challenge (because of course that is what a song often is: a battle cry, a terrace chant, a come-and-have-a-go-if-you-think-you're-hard-enough). The bird-catchers knew this. Standard practice was to take a captive singing chaffinch into the countryside ('Nosey' Warren plied his trade in the parks of Highgate) and prompt it to let rip with a *chuck-wee-do*. Any resident cock-chaffinch will waste no time in mak-ing his presence felt – 'just the same as you or any other fellow might who caught a strange cove a whistlin' round your lodgin's where you and your missus lived', 'Nosey' explained.

The caged singer was kept concealed under a cloth; a stuffed bird was used to complete the illusion of an

interloper on the wild chaffinch's turf. The careful place-
ment of twigs smeared with sticky lime did the rest. It
was said that a bird-catcher might, using these perfidious
means and moving from spot to spot, bag between fifty
and seventy chaffinches in a single day.

Today, there is no UK trade in wild chaffinches; traffic in any birds taken from the wild is prohibited under
the Wildlife and Countryside Act 1981. The heyday of
vinkensport is long since over – but chaffinches are not
the only birds, and there is more to competitive birdsong
than *susk-e-wiet* and *chuck-wee-do*.

In Malaysia, the zebra dove, *Geopelia striata*, is known
as the merbok; in the Philippines it is the kurokutok, and
in Indonesia it is the perkutut. All of these names derive
from the bird's call, a soft, agreeable, staccato five-note
whistle (having listened to recordings of the sound,
I might have called it a *hu-huhu-hoo-hoo* myself). It's a
nice-looking bird, with smartly barred plumage and a delicate head – more like a collared dove than a woodpigeon
– and it's pretty common in the scrub and farmland of
its native south-east Asia. It's not rare, but it is treasured.

Zebra-dove singing contests are fundamental to the
culture of the Chana district of southern Thailand. Bird
fanciers are known as *chawawong*; contests may involve
dozens of doves, suspended in cages from high poles.

The doves are judged not on the speed of their delivery but on the beauty and power of their call (here the syllables are rendered *wow-ta-kong*).

The cooing of the zebra dove is an aural emblem of Chana. It's more than birdsong; it's intertwined with the culture, economy and well-being of the district. In the late 1990s, a Thai government initiative to boost industry in the south of the country (part of the 'Indonesia–Malaysia–Thailand Growth Triangle') saw the construction of a new power station, power line and gas separation plant in Chana. A familiar pattern of industrial fallout followed: marine life declined; farmers' crop yields suffered. Most potently of all, the voice of the zebra dove was, many thought, in danger.

'The call of the zebra dove is a fragile thing,' said campaigner Adun Jema. 'The quality of their sound is affected by chillies and mosquito spray, so just imagine how much it deteriorates with factory smoke, fumes and construction waste. The temperature, water quality and noise levels all influence the bird calls. If their sound quality is low, their value depreciates. We're left with birds worth no more than 100 *baht*. This is why we added our voices to the protests.'

A settlement was eventually reached: the owners of the industrial plants pledged to sponsor the *chawawong* of

Chana to the tune of 1.5 million *baht*. The money was put towards an annual zebra-dove singing contest.

James Greenwood remarks acidly that the bird fancier 'has a proper contempt for Nature as an altogether incompetent party in works of creation'. The pre-Romantic notion of nature as something to be improved upon – by cropping a terrier's ears, say, or burning a chaffinch's eyes – clung on in the Victorian East End. The drawing-rooms of the gentry, too, persisted in the belief that birdsong, though diverting, was far from a finished product; having a pet songbird was all very well, but how *dull*, my dear, for a songbird to sing nothing but birdsong all day long.*

We've talked about the ways in which musicians have tried to incorporate birdsong in their concertos and symphonies; in the eighteenth century, building on the notion of the inherent superiority of *our* music – and, of course, for the fun of it – the fashionable thing to do was to train one's bird to learn humansong.

---

* This view of the natural world as a concept with much room for improvement was embodied by the eighteenth-century French painter François Boucher, famous for remarking that nature was 'too green, and badly lit'.

John Walsh's book *The Bird Fancyer's Delight* was published in around 1715; it was a collection of music for the flageolet and flute, tailored to suit the vocal talents of various popular songbirds: 'canary-bird', linnet, bullfinch, woodlark, blackbird, thrush, nightingale and starling. Beginning when the bird was very young, you played the tunes (including gavottes, marches and preludes) to your bird, and soon – in theory – the bird would sing them back to you ('The blackbird', for instance, 'will learn any easy tune that is played to him on a flute or other wind instrument, and whistle it accurately.')

Later, ingenious French bird fanciers developed the 'serinette', a tiny crank-powered barrel organ that played rudimentary tunes in the favoured key of a given cage bird. Its purpose was to give the flageolet-player a rest, and provide an automated means of teaching birds new songs by rote.

The idea was to create something completely synthetic, exclusively artificial; in stark contrast to the Cockney chaffinch-keepers, taking to the shrubberies to give their birds a refresher course in *chuck-wee-do* and so on, Walsh's readers were urged to keep their birds from being exposed to *any* wild song – it would only, so to speak, mess with their programming. One's canary or bullfinch was to act as a living music-box, and nothing more.

The canary's ability to pick up new melodies was one of the reasons for its widespread and persistent popularity. Bullfinches, too, had long been known to be especially adept learners: German foresters were whistling to their tame bullfinches – and the bullfinches were whistling back – long before the serinette came along. In the nineteenth century, Charles Darwin heard of a bullfinch that had been trained to whistle a German waltz, and had been sold for ten guineas as a consequence. 'When this bird was first introduced into a room where other birds were kept and he began to sing,' Darwin wrote, 'all the others, consisting of about twenty linnets and canaries, ranged themselves on the nearest side of their cages, and listened with the greatest interest to the new performer.'

Starlings were also featured in *The Bird Fancyer's Delight*, but to a modern ear they might be thought of as an odd choice of pet: too raucous, too raffish, too rakishly downmarket. They are, however, terrific singers, unpredictable and zany; they're also first-class mimics (as anyone who's been tricked by a starling's car-alarm impersonation will confirm). One starling, purchased at a Viennese pet shop in 1784 for 34 *kreutzer*, had an enviable music teacher: one Wolfgang Amadeus Mozart, who immediately taught it to whistle the opening of his Piano Concerto No. 17 in G (but noted that the starling sang in G sharp instead of G). The starling lived with the Mozarts for three years, and was buried with great ceremony when it passed on.

This kind of thing was a high point in the humanisation of songbirds. There was very little left of the wild in these well-kept, keenly drilled birds – at least, that was the idea. But the high profile of the cage bird in society had a double-edged effect: the painstaking refinement of the pet finch or starling served as a reminder, for some, of what had been lost (or, rather, stolen away). For every middle-class bird fancier delighted with their *oiseau chantant*, there was a socially conscious novelist hearing a cry for liberty in the captive's song.

Caged birds are everywhere in the fiction of the eighteenth and nineteenth centuries. The high-gloss gilt of the baroque era was being rubbed off; affected artificiality was passing out of fashion. Freedom was the new watchword: William Blake, the great Romantic pioneer, famously wrote in around 1803 that 'a Robin Redbreast in a Cage / Puts all Heaven in a Rage'.

The novels of Charles Dickens are full of captives: workers trapped by the iniquities of industry and commerce; innocents struggling in the webs of law and Chancery; women enslaved or stultified by social convention. Dickens' birds reflect that: in *Dombey and Son*, the ghastly Mr Carker keeps a parrot, 'swinging in the gilded hoop within her gaudy cage' and reminding us of poor Edith Dombey's married misery; mad old Miss Flite in *Bleak House* declares that her larks, linnets and goldfinches – 'Hope', 'Joy', 'Peace', 'Madness', 'Folly' and 'Jargon' among them – will be released only when her intolerably long-running lawsuit is settled.

Caged bullfinches, with their regimented melodies, turn up in two significant novels about the role of women in middle-class courtship. In Frances Burney's *Camilla* (1796), the heroine is disturbed by the bird-keeper's brutality ('Everything's the better for a little beating, as I tells my wife', he remarks); when the cruel Alphonso Bellamy, having bullied Camilla's good-hearted sister Eugenia into marrying him, threatens to 'lock [her] up on bread and water for the rest of [her] life', it's hard not to see a parallel.

Maria Edgeworth's *Belinda* (1857), meanwhile, deploys a stray bullfinch's learned whistle as a clever plot device (the bird's 'very particular tune, which I never heard any bullfinch, or any human creature, sing anything like before' is used to reunite the bird with its owner, with dramatic consequences), but again, the motifs of captivity – the owner of the bullfinch, for instance, is said to have 'a most beautiful young creature there [in her home], shut up, who has been seduced' – suggest a wider social agenda.

Most affecting of all, for me, is a bird that appears in Laurence Sterne's 1768 travel novel *A Sentimental Journey*. Sterne's narrator, Yorick, meets a caged starling in Paris, while musing on the notorious Bastille jail (it would be stormed, and France consumed by revolution, some twenty years later).

'I can't get out—I can't get out,' said the starling. I stood looking at the bird: and to every person who came through the passage it ran fluttering to the side towards which they approach'd it, with the same lamentation of its captivity—'I can't get out,' said the starling.

—God help thee! said I, but I'll let thee out, cost what it will; so I turn'd about the cage to get to the door; it was twisted and double twisted so fast with wire, there was no getting it open without pulling the cage to pieces—I took both hands to it.

The bird flew to the place where I was attempting his deliverance, and thrusting his head through the trellis, press'd his breast against it, as if impatient.—I fear, poor creature! said I, I cannot set thee at liberty.—'No,' said the starling—'I can't get out—I can't get out,' said the starling.

'I vow I never had my affections more tenderly awakened,' Yorick – in fact Sterne, thinly veiled – concludes. 'Disguise thyself as thou wilt, still, slavery! said I—still thou art a bitter draught! and though thousands in all ages have been made to drink of thee, thou art no less bitter on that account.'

The song of birds – like the flight of birds, with which it is so often intertwined – speaks to us of freedom. Keeping a songbird in a cage feels a bit paradoxical: why would you take a living symbol of liberty and lock it behind bars? But with song (unlike with flight), the paradox isn't complete, because, of course, cage or no cage, the song goes on – and that, I suppose, is for us the sound, not of freedom, but of hope.

6

A Hush Descends

The wheatlands are green, snow and frost are away,

Birds, why are ye silent on such a sweet day?

– John Clare, 'Birds, Why Are Ye Silent?' (1840s)

Warnings, in the bird world, take many forms. Jays are among the most vigilant birds in the woodland: a harsh *kaaugh* – or several *kaaughs*, as a jay community passes on the message – means there's trouble afoot. The throaty machine-gunning of a magpie tells you the same thing. A robin lisps sharply, or shouts *tick!*; anxious swallows – which, according to the bird writer Conor Mark Jameson, 'will alarm-call at a passing cloud' – send out a panicky series of *che-WEE* calls. Alarm calls can act as a kind of universal language among songbirds: whereas a wren's ear-splitting song, for instance, will have no effect on a song thrush, each bird will respond briskly to the other's alarm call. This, of course, benefits both parties (it's never a bad idea to learn how to shout 'Fire!' in a foreign language) – but there's another reason for these emergency outbreaks of mutual understanding. Alarm calls have evolved to disguise the location of the caller; the idea is that the crow or stoat or cat should find it hard to tell where the noise is coming from. Acoustically, this means that the calls should be high-pitched, pure in tone and rising in volume – and so they are, taking such similar forms (on a sonogram, they look like a family of closely related worms) that their meaning is clear even across species boundaries.

Another kind of warning is even more universally understood.

'A sudden hush,' Helen Macdonald calls it in *H Is for Hawk*. The American naturalist Sarah Hubbard describes it as a 'cone of silence'. A hawk is on the prowl in the forest; the singing, the chirping, the companionable contact-calling stops. No one makes a sound.

Hubbard recalls the visit of a Cooper's hawk* to her local woods in Athens, Georgia. 'The only sound was that of the crickets, and even their song was chilling to the bone,' she writes. 'There was a chickadee hanging out

---

* A formidable bird of prey – fast, powerful, agile; bigger than a sparrowhawk, smaller than a goshawk – native to woodlands across the US. It has an alarm call of its own: a rapid *yik-yik-yik* that sounds not unlike an angry monkey.

near me, and I could see her shivering and feel that same fear in my body.'

Jon Young, in his book *What the Robin Knows*, describes a similar occasion in coastal California: 'Almost all of the birds across the entire valley – robins, song sparrows, juncos, Bewick's wrens, golden-crowned and white-crowned sparrows, California and spotted towhees, scrub jays and Steller's jays, flickers, ruby-crowed kinglets, chestnut-backed chickadees and California quail, to name most of the players – fall into silence when a Cooper's flies in.'

I've seen it myself, in England: a feeding party of long-tailed tits cuts off its familiar hubbub of zinging *tsees* and *tsirrups* and drops from the birch canopy as if gravity has been suddenly doubled. They sit tight and silent in the woodland understorey until the sparrowhawk has passed overhead.

A silent forest is a frightened forest – a forest under threat.

Most of these freezes last only a few moments – until the hawk has gone away (or until someone has been eaten). But what if they lasted a lot longer than that – for years, say, or decades? What if, in fact, the birdsong never came back at all? And what if we weren't just talking about one patch of forest, one sparrowhawk's territory, but *all* the forest, and not just the forest but the farmland, too, and the moors, and the suburban back-gardens, and the riverside reed beds, and the city rooftops?

Some numbers to consider. Between 1995 and 2013, the UK skylark population fell by 24 per cent ('fell' doesn't seem quite adequate; 'plummeted', 'crashed'?). That's a lot of 'shrill delight' missing from our meadows. Numbers of willow tits and marsh tits – twin forest for-agers, buff-grey and black-capped* – dropped by 81 and 29 per cent over the same period: an awful lot of *pee-chay*s, *tsi-tsi*s, *chip-chip*s and *tiu tiu*s stripped out of our broadleaf woodland. Greenfinch, burly, frowning, sounding like a 'gruff canary' in the words of one bird book, down 32 per cent; mistle thrush, once known as the 'stormcock' for the delight it seems to find in belting out a song in the teeth of a spring gale, down 31 per cent; linnet down 29 per cent, corn bunting down 40 per cent, meadow pipit down 15 per cent; garden warbler, maestro of a sweet, wild note to rival the blackcap, down 19 per cent.

The population of nightingales in Britain dropped by 37 per cent, and really doesn't have much further to fall. In the mid-twentieth century, the writer Aldous

---

* Graham Shortt offered me another ID tip here, based on the relative tidiness of the marsh tit's plumage: 'Marsh is off to work; willow is just back from a three-day rock festival.'

Huxley remarked to his brother, the zoologist Julian, that 'we are losing half the subject matter of English poetry', which remains true, but is only a brushstroke in the bigger picture. In a piece for the *New Statesman* in 2015, Helen Macdonald argued that 'not everyone has read Keats and Clare, and nightingales do not speak to me of poetry at all. They are simply astonishing, in and of themselves.' Losing the nightingale, she went on, would 'constitute a thinning of human experience, a shrinking of the available meanings of spring'. Not to mention the even more severe thinning of nightingale experience – not, as we've seen, that the nightingales really have time to fret about that.

I do worry about the diminution that we all suffer, that *everything* suffers, when songbirds – and bird songs – are driven from our country. Our lives become less rich. The world's patterns lose some of their intricacy. But what bothers me more is not so much that this happens as that we *let* it happen.

Some songbird declines simply aren't our fault. Whitethroat numbers tumbled in the late 1960s because of a severe drought in their wintering grounds south of the Sahara; short of organising some sort of whitethroat Live Aid, there wasn't a great deal we could do about that. The songbird apocalypse that Rachel Carson described in her world-changing 1962 book *Silent Spring* – when one Norfolk landowner reported that his estate was 'like a battlefield' littered with 'innumerable corpses, including masses of small birds' – was attributable to the use in agriculture of murderously toxic seed-dressings, now widely banned. Our modern-day bird populations still carry the dents and scars from these events and others like them, but these are artefacts, from another time, inked in the debit columns of a previous generation.

The declines of the last twenty years, though – these are *ours*.

What complicates matters is that we might not even really hear the silence, on account of all the noise.

In 2013, scientists in the Canadian city of Edmonton identified a curious pattern in the diversity levels of the city's songbirds (which range from black-capped chickadees, purveyors of a marvellously clean-edged 'pee-pee-pee' call, to purple finches, once described as resembling 'a sparrow dipped in raspberry juice'). Low levels of species diversity were found to correlate not with fragmented habitat or food shortages, but with noise. The deep rumble of traffic, in particular, smothered the songs and calls of birds that operate within the same low-frequency band. Without an audible song, male birds were crippled, unable to stake out territory or advertise for mates. Breeding rates, as a result, dropped. Researchers have seen similar patterns by the side of German *autobahn*s and in the US Rocky Mountains.

It's not just about being heard; it's also about hearing others. Urban areas present a unique suite of threats for songbirds (one of them, our little tortoiseshell cat Hedy, is kipping under my desk as I write this). The dense networks of noise that grow up within our cities make it near-impossible for a sparrow to pick out, for instance, a blackbird's alarm call or the giveaway tinkle of a cat's bell. Studies of chaffinches have shown that birds in noisy districts spend less time feeding, and more time keeping an eye out for predators. If you want to imagine what life must be like for a small bird in a noisy city, put on a blindfold and take a slow walk across the Hanger Lane gyratory.

Some birds adapt, of course. It's what wild things do: adapt, or die.

It's thought that some urban birds begin singing earlier in the day than they usually would, in order to beat the traffic and get in ahead of rush hour (but in cities where rush hour seems to extend from seven in the morning to ten at night, like London or Brussels or LA, this strategy might run into trouble). The robins, blackbirds, blue tits and chaffinches that live under the flightpaths outside Berlin-Tegel airport reschedule their dawn choruses according to the airport's take-off times. City great tits in the Netherlands have been found to increase the frequency of their calls. In downtown Berlin, nightingales sing more loudly, cranking up their volume in an attempt to compete with the cars, buses and *Straßenbahn*. Nightingales have the vocal kit to do that; many birds don't.

The resilience of nature – its bouncebackability, as an American sportscaster might put it – goes only so far. It's not just change but the *pace* of change – the suddenness of dogs and rats spilling from an adventurer's ship onto a Pacific island, of a city of skyscrapers springing up from swampland or desert, of climate change more rapid than any seen before in our planet's history – that does the damage.

Bernie Krause warned about the impact of the 'anthropophony' – human noise – on bird biophonies in *The Great Animal Orchestra*. First a passing aeroplane prompts the birds he is hearing to 'quieten down to almost nothing'; then a helicopter buzzes by ('The birds become quiet again; really silent this time.') 'Human-generated noise affects entire biophonies,' he writes. In the Sequoia forests of California, 'even distant noise-producing mechanisms interrupted the dawn chorus of many biomes within earshot, all at the same moment'.

In our exchange of emails, Krause told me that the 'silent spring' that Rachel Carson warned us about (and that ecologists have seldom stopped warning us about since) had already happened – in 2015, and just a twenty-minute drive from his northern California home.

'It was the only time I've witnessed such a phenomenon anywhere on the planet', he said. But this isn't quite the kind of silence Carson was writing about. That was a silence of empty woodlands, denuded farmland, a ravaged countryside – the aftermath of a songbird holocaust wrought by reckless agribusiness. Krause's silence, by contrast, was about what had happened to birdsong itself. In a habitat stressed to breaking point by human recklessness, it had been mugged, suffocated, cowed into quietness.

'There were lots of birds present,' Krause says. 'But not a single song or call.'

The biologist Bridget Stutchbury reaches for an apt metaphor when she writes about songbird populations in her book *Silence of the Songbirds*: the canary in the mine.

As we've seen, miners have been using caged canaries for centuries to guard against poisonous gases: when carbon monoxide reaches a hazardous level, the canary conks out. Looking at the stats – the recent steep falls in numbers of migratory US songbirds such as the eastern kingbird, Kentucky warbler and bobolink – Stutchbury concludes that what we have here is a dead canary.

But actually it's worse than that. Stutchbury points out that the death of a miner's canary didn't make things *worse* – it was simply a singing CO meter, a warning about how bad things were. With songbirds, it's a different matter. Songbirds are a key component in the very systems they're warning us about; they carry out essential maintenance, like controlling insect pests, distributing seeds and moving nutrients through the food chain (take a look at the pavements of Rome after a megaflock of starlings has passed through and you'll get an idea of just how many nutrients they can move).

'The world around us is already in a very fragile state, barely hanging on by a thread,' Stutchbury writes. 'We cannot afford to lose our birds.'

Ecology is complicated. It's *meant* to be complicated – the more complicated the better. Ecology is the science of webs, networks; there are seldom any easy answers. What is killing our birdsong (and not only our birdsong:

also the *kirrri-nggk* of the grey partridge, as though some-one has grabbed the bird by the throat part-way through; also the bubbles and wails of the curlew, more common now in books about the uplands than in the uplands themselves; also the rook's *caw*; also the wild *waheys* of the lapwing)?*

I don't know how much we should blame inten-sive farming (changes in land use, new patterns of crop management, pesticides and inorganic fertilisers); I don't know how much to blame the winnowing of our wood-lands and the drainage of our wetlands, or pollution, or the insistent lichen-like spread of our towns and cities.†But I do think these things can be bundled together under a single heading: neglect.

Maybe we don't care because we don't see or hear the birds around us; maybe we don't see or hear them

---

* It was once said that lapwings were the cursed souls of those who taunted Jesus Christ on his way to Golgotha. That's never sat right with me: lapwings – whooping and wheeling and dive-bombing on pied, spoony wings – always look to be having far too much *fun*.
† I *do* know, by the way, how much we should blame egg-thieving, nestling-murdering magpies: not at all. Contrary to the rot they run in the tabloids, magpies – like all predators – are *part* of the ecosystem; they're a cog in the machine. Problems only arise when ecosystems become unbalanced, by abrupt or drastic change. Quiz question: what's got two opposable thumbs and a habit of imposing drastic change on ecosystems?

because we don't care. Maybe we just think that other things are more important (George Osborne, when he was Chancellor, described breeding nightingales as 'feathered obstacles' to economic growth – goodness, we're a long way from Clare and Coleridge now).

Or maybe it's not that we don't want to listen – it's that we've forgotten how it's done. I suspect that this has been a problem for longer than we care to admit.

Kurt Fristrup, a senior scientist at the US National Park Service, has called it 'learned deafness'.

'We are conditioning ourselves to ignore the infor-mation coming into our ears,' he told a meeting of the American Association for the Advancement of Science in 2015. 'This gift that we are born with – to reach out and hear things hundreds of metres away, all these incredible sounds – is in danger of being lost through a generational amnesia.' It's a twofold threat: 'There is a real danger, both of loss of auditory acuity, where we are exposed to noise for so long that we stop listening, but also a loss of listening habits, where we lose the ability to engage with the environment the way we were built to.'

Our hearing deteriorates quickly enough as it is. Earlier this year, the warden at my local patch admitted to me that he could no longer pick out the top-notes of the long-tailed tits: 'Too much punk music, too many years working with chainsaws,' he said ruefully. In 1774, Gilbert White – though not known to have been a punk fan – wrote sadly of his encroaching deafness: 'I lose all the pleasing notices and little intimations arising from rural sounds; and May is as silent and mute with respect to the notes of the birds as August.' To just *give up* on listening feels like a dereliction.

We don't *have* to hear music in birdsong. We're allowed to think it's a mad racket, a clattering noise, a damnable disturbance* – but I think we should try to notice it. It's a part of our world – both the world in which we evolved, the world of forest and savannah, heath and seashore, the world of the wild, and the world we've built up around ourselves: our human culture. It's a part of us.

I wonder about where all this culture fits in – all the poetry, all the music, the meditations, the potent

---

* It might, indeed, drive us mad, as the song of the common hawk-cuckoo or 'brain-fever bird' was said to do: 'The song of the brain-fever demon starts on a low but steadily rising key,' wrote Mark Twain in *Following the Equator* (1897), 'and is a spiral twist which augments in intensity and severity with each added spiral, growing sharper and sharper, and more and more painful, more and more agonizing, more and more maddening, intolerable, unendurable, as it bores deeper and deeper and deeper into the listener's brain, until at last the brain fever comes as a relief and the man dies. I am bringing some of these birds home to America.'

sonic iconography of birdsong. How has it affected the way we think about real-life birds? It's deepened our attachment to them, I'm sure, but I worry that it's made us complacent. We sometimes talk about a place or a person or a bird song being 'immortalised in verse'; I worry that we take that a little bit too literally. All this effort we've gone to to capture birdsong, in art, in music, in vaudeville impersonations, in sonograms and wax cylinders – do we think that we've put birdsong out of danger, preserved it, set it safely in glass like a flower in a paperweight? As long as we have a *Works of Wordsworth* on the bookshelf, we'll have cuckoos. As long as we can call up a Respighi piece on Spotify, we'll have nightingales.

It doesn't work like that, of course. Birdsong is dynamic and ongoing; nature isn't a museum but a churning mill of individuals, species, climates and habitats. We shouldn't forget that – I worry that we will, though, if we don't keep listening to the birds.

Will we even notice if our birds fall silent?

We'll notice eventually, I think. John Keats, you'll remember, had an instinctive response to birdsong, a deep-brain reflex that bypassed thousands of years of evolution. I think something similar happens when the birds go quiet. We know what it means.

Helen Dickson told me that film-makers will sometimes deliberately cut out birdsong to create a feeling
of dread and doom (as in, for instance, John Hillcoat's
post-apocalyptic 2009 drama *The Road*) – audiences
notice, without being told, that something is wrong.
We've seen how the birds stopped singing for Thomas
Hardy's Tess when the world turned against her.

Even more suggestive of a world gone awry,
nature out of joint, is 'The Pike's Song' of 1928, by the
Finnish poet Aaro Hellaakoski. In this poem, a pike – a
duckling-snatching predatory fish – climbs a tree, and
begins to sing, so wildly that 'birds fell silent / immediately / as if overcome by / the waters' weight / and
lonesomeness' / cold embrace'. It's a profoundly strange
vision from another poet who knew the natural world
well (Hellaakoski was a geographer by trade); the suffocated silence of the birds is central to the deep-seated
sense of unease.

More recently, in Denise Levertov's 'Sound of the
Axe', the birds cease to sing because the 'world-tree' is
about to be felled: 'The birds were silent. Why? she said.
/ Thunder, they told her, / thunder is coming.' Another
elemental threat, looming like a blue-black storm cloud;
another intimation of something bad coming our way.
And Keats himself used the same trick: the first stanza

of his 'La Belle Dame Sans Merci' ends with four cold, thudding syllables: 'And no birds sing.'

These writers and film-makers understood what we all half-consciously know: what a silent spring means to us, deep down, in the part of us that remembers how wild things work. Quiet birds are bad news.

So I think we'll notice, eventually, as our springs fall silent. The question is whether we'll notice in time to do something about it.

There are apps for identifying bird songs now, and I think that's great; there's xeno-canto, and the RSPB website, and a hundred other resources to help you tell a *chet* from a *whet* from a *wheet* from a *tweet* – or, for that matter, a *tack* from a *chack*. Does technology distance us from nature? It doesn't have to. It can, on the contrary, give us a direct line through to the wild world; it can keep alive our engagement with the way things really are, the way birds really sing. It can help us to *listen* (what you do with what you hear is up to you).

I still find it hard to pick out a treecreeper's call in an April woodland. I think that trying, though, is worth the effort.

This makes me think of a moment in the gentle BBC television sitcom *Detectorists*. Metal-detector enthusiast Lance worries that, in unearthing a valuable Saxon trinket, he has brought down a curse on himself; that he has disturbed the natural currents of the countryside, and forfeited his connection with nature. 'I've started stumbling over rocks and tripping into nettles and I can't remember birdsong any more,' he complains. No spoilers here: he makes amends, I won't say how, but once he has done so a ripple of birdsong sounds in the background. 'Blackbird,' says Lance, correctly, and smiles.

Detectorists feels like a very English programme. The first episode opens with a skylark's song (pleasingly, the species is precisely specified in the script by the writer and co-star, Mackenzie Crook). Birdsong and place are, as we've seen, closely interlocked; both offer us a feeling of continuity – but both, like everything else, are subject to change, too. And both have a habit of telling us back our own tales.

I've paid a lot of attention to the birds around me since I started researching this book. Well, I've always done that – since I was a nine-year-old getting overexcited about a siskin on the bird-feeder – but this time I've been listening, too. The duelling robins at the railway station. The autumn dipper zooting and honking on the weir. The medley of dinky finches in the high sycamores opposite my mum and dad's house. The blackcap in the hedgerow. Once you start listening, the stuff is suddenly *everywhere*.

I still think that there's more babble than beauty in birdsong. I'm allowed to think that and still think it's wonderful.

Further Reading

Prologue

In so many ways, the story of birdsong study in Britain began with Gilbert White's *Natural History of Selborne* (there are many editions available – the 2014 edition from Little Toller has an introduction by James Lovelock and illustrations by Eric Ravilious). Richard Mabey's 2006 biography of White (from Profile Books) fills in valuable context.

The bird impersonator Percy Edwards told his story in his memoir *The Road I Travelled* (Arthur Barker, 1979). It's no longer in print, but second-hand copies aren't hard to find.

You can find out more about the University of Aberdeen's splendid Listening to Birds project – and delve into a rich repository of birdsong experience – at: http://www .abdn.ac.uk/birdsong/about/.

Chapter 1: An Infinity of Possibilities

Edward Grey's *The Charm of Birds* has deservedly gone through dozens of reprints – my copy is a 1931 edition from Hodder & Stoughton, with woodcuts by Robert Gibbings. *The Life of the Robin* by David Lack – first published in 1943 – was reissued in 2016 by Pallas Athene, with a new introduction by David Lindo ('the Urban Birder'), illustrations by Robert Gillmor and postscripts from biologist David Harper and Peter Lack, David's son. And you can find out more about the nefarious and complicated cuckoo in Nick Davies' *Cuckoo: Cheating by Nature* (Bloomsbury, 2015).

If you're looking for an overview of birds in literature, *Birds in Literature* by Leonard Lutwack (University Press of Florida, 1994) fits the bill: wide-ranging, smart and insightful. *The Poetry of Birds*, a Viking anthology edited by Tim Dee and Simon Armitage, is a terrific treasury of bird-themed verse that includes many of the poems mentioned in this book (Hardy's 'The Blinded Bird' and Wordsworth's 'To the Cuckoo' among them).

John Bevis's *The Keartons: Inventing Nature Photography* (Uniformbooks, 2016) explores the work of the pioneering brothers with intelligence and verve. And Richard Dawkins' *Unweaving the Rainbow* (I have the 1999 Penguin edition) is a vigorous defence of science in response to John Keats's complaint that 'all charms fly / At the mere touch of cold philosophy'.

Chapter 2: A Song of Many Parts

In researching the history of how we've made scientific sense of birdsong, I was indebted to two weighty books: *Ten Thousand Birds: Ornithology Since Darwin* by Tim Birkhead, Jo Wimpenny and Bob Montgomerie (Princeton University Press, 2014) and *Nature's Music: The Science of Birdsong* (Elsevier Academic Press, 2004) by Peter Marler and Hans Slabbekoorn.

Born to Sing by Charles Hartshorne (I have the 1992 Indiana UP edition) and *Why Birds Sing: A Journey into the Mystery of Birdsong* by David Rothenberg (Basic Books, 2006) are both classics of birdsong writing. John Bevis (him again) packed an amazing amount of fascinating information into his book *Aaaaw to Zzzzzd: The Words of Birds* (MIT Press, 2010).

Amy Clampitt's 'Syrinx' is included in the 1999 *Collected Poems* from Penguin Random House. And the many works of H. Mortimer Batten may be found in fusty second-hand bookshops the length and breadth of England.

Chapter 3: Coming Home

Paul Fussell's *The Great War and Modern Memory* is a magnificent exploration of what the First World War did to us, and how, in the years since, we have remembered and mythologised it. I first read it in the 1977 OUP paperback when I was a student, but I'd unhesitatingly recommend the 2009 illustrated version from Sterling.

George Seaver's *Edward Wilson, Nature Lover* – his affectionate portrait of the great ornithologist, artist and Antarctic explorer – is out of print; Isobel Williams' *With Scott in the Antarctic: Edward Wilson* (The History Press, 2008) is a more recent biography.

I was grateful to Penelope Vigar's *The Novels of Thomas Hardy: Illusion and Reality* (Athlone Press, 1974) for her insights on birdsong in *Tess of the D'Urbervilles*, and to Delia Da Sousa Correa's chapter on song in *Adam Bede* in *George Eliot in Context* (Margaret Harris, ed.); Cambridge University Press, 2013).

The books of Bernie Krause are must-reads for anyone wishing to learn more about the under-studied field of natural acoustics. *The Great Animal Orchestra* (Profile, 2012) was my way in to Krause's work.

You can read more about Dr Rupert Marshall's research into corn-bunting dialects at: http://users.aber.ac.uk/rmm/cornbuntings.htm.

Chapter 4: An Elusive Song

Elizabeth Eva Leach's *Sung Birds: Music, Nature & Poetry in the Later Middle Ages* (Cornell University Press, 2007) is an absorbing and scholarly study of how, in the formative years of modern music, birdsong fitted into our ideas of what was and wasn't musical.

Walter Garstang's *Songs of the Birds* (1935) is good fun to read. Richard Jefferies described his song-filled wanderings near The Waffrons in *The Hills and the Vale* (1909); *Landscape With Figures*, a 2013 Penguin collection of Jefferies' writings edited and introduced by Richard Mabey, is a great introduction to this multifaceted writer's work.

Beatrice Harrison's memoir *The Cello and the Nightingales*, published in 1985, presents the cellist as a dedicated musician and an engagingly dizzy writer (her editor, Patricia Cleveland-Peck, admitted to having to pare back Harrison's 'frequent superlatives and adjectives of endearment').

You can read Alison Greggor's wonderful 'Why Can't We Love Like an Albatross?' at: http://kingsreview.co.uk/articles/why-cant-we-love-like-an-albatross/.

Chapter 5: A Captive Melody

Mark Cocker's *Birds Britannica* (with Richard Mabey; Chatto & Windus, 2005) – for my money, one of the finest bird books ever put together – provided me with terrific material on the culture of chaffinch competition. So too did the work of James Greenwood, 'the Amateur Casual': there are editions of his 1874 book *In Strange Company* out there, but I discovered his work through Lee Jackson's superb Victorian London website: http://www.victorianlondon.org/.

The Bird Fancyer's Delight, composer Sarah Angliss's 2011 documentary for BBC Radio 4, takes a hugely entertaining and informative look at the training of caged songbirds; at the time of writing it was still available at: http://www .bbc.co.uk/programmes/b0128pyp (it includes the endearing titbit that ornithologist Geoff Sample whistles the opening riff of Arthur Conley's 'Sweet Soul Music' to the blackbirds in his garden).

Frances Burney's *Camilla*, Maria Edgeworth's *Belinda* and Laurence Sterne's *A Sentimental Journey* are all available in the Oxford World's Classics series.

Chapter 6: A Hush Descends

Rachel Carson's *Silent Spring* was first published in 1962 and is rightly remembered not only as a classic work of conservation writing but as a major turning-point in the history of the environmental movement. In 2012, the British wildlife writer Conor Mark Jameson produced a follow-up, *Silent Spring Revisited* (Bloomsbury), which offers an up-to-date take on the same troubling subject; Bridget Stutchbury's excellent *Silence of the Songbirds* (Walker Books, 2007) tackles the question from a US perspective. Helen Macdonald's *H Is for Hawk* (Jonathan Cape, 2014) needs no introduction from me.

And both series of *Detectorists* are available to buy on DVD or via download from the BBC: http://www.bbc.co.uk/programmes/b06l51nr/products.

Acknowledgements

No one who writes a book of this sort does so alone. I didn't, anyway. From start to finish I was reliant on the insight, knowledge and generosity of a whole load of other people. Some were already friends; others didn't know me from Adam. I'm hugely grateful to them all.

Let's name names. I would never have got to write this book without the support of Matt Merritt (who also, getting on for ten years ago, commissioned my first article as a freelancer, and therefore has a lot to answer for). And I wouldn't be writing about nature for a living without the help of Mark Cocker, Anne-Marie Conway, Ben Hoare and Steve Warrillow.

Several brilliant people took the time to speak to me and to come up with intelligent answers to my vague, stumbling questions; in doing so, they made this book a dozen times better than it would otherwise have been. Heartfelt thanks to Elizabeth Eva Leach, Graham Shortt, Bernie Krause, Helen Dickson, Dr Peter Tickle and Brian Briggs.

The list of people who contributed in other ways to *A Sweet, Wild Note* is a long one. In no particular order,

Acknowledgements

I would like to say thank you to Steve Rutt, Nic Allan, Vanessa Woolf, Tim Lozinski, Gethin Jones, Helen Macdonald, Lee Jackson, Paddy Bullard, Owen Shirley, Dan Stowell, Heidi Stiene, Sophie Coulombeau and Clare Heal. The staff of the Leeds Library and the British Library at Boston Spa also deserve the highest praise, (a) for helping me write this book and (b) just generally.

Jennie Condell and Pippa Crane, my wonderful editors at Elliott & Thompson, were endlessly supportive throughout the writing process and did a terrific job of knocking my drafts into shape. Lynn Hatzius's stunning cover design, Tim Oakenfull's illustrations and Linden Lawson's all-seeing copy-editing transformed my manuscript into the fine-looking book you now hold in your hands. Thanks to them all.

I want to thank my mum and dad – for all those bird books, all those drives out to Pugneys and Fairburn Ings, among so much else – and I want to remember my granddad, Arthur Heaton: without him and his hardback *AA Book of British Birds* I don't think I'd ever have been a birdwatcher.

Finally, the biggest of all imaginable thank yous to my wife, Frin, who amazes me, and makes everything possible.

Index

Index

Index

Index